SHEEPDOG

The Story of a Working Border Collie

TOSS

ROY SAUNDERS

Sheepdog Glory

THE STORY OF A WORKING BORDER COLLIE

Illustrated by the author

OUTRUN PRESS

Cover photo by Denise Wall.

ISBN-13: 978-0-9794690-2-2
ISBN-10: 0-9794690-2-3

Library of Congress Control Number: 2008938470

CONTENTS

ILLUSTRATIONS

PHOTOGRAPHS

(between pages 72–73)

The greatest test: Toss has been called up to within eight inches of a cornered sheep, and still keeps his head.

Toss keeps the flock in position while one of the sheep is caught.

A piece of wire entangled with the wool has to be clipped off.

Over the sticks

Flock inspection

Driving practice for the trials

Penning practice for the trials

PREFACE
by David Rees

It is a privilege to be asked to write a preface for the reprinted edition of *Sheepdog Glory*. I was fortunate enough
to have met Roy Saunders in the 1970s, when he was an
elderly gentleman and I was a young man in a hurry, from a
different generation, about to embark on an unbelievable
walk down the avenues of this wonderful pastime of ours. I
was immediately impressed with Roy Saunders' incredible
enthusiasm for all things associated with the Border Collie
in particular and with nature, in its widest aspect, in
general. Roy Saunders was the consummate naturalist;
he was incredibly aware of everything that lived and
breathed and moved in the countryside. His knowledge of
the Border Collie, and its history and genealogy, impressed
me immediately and instilled in me the desire to emulate
that knowledge. I like to think some of his enthusiasm
rubbed off on me.

Roy Saunders was articulate and intelligent. His writing,
although tinged with romanticism, serves as a historical
reference for those of us who continually research the
history of the Border Collie. The pen portraits he paints of
men like J. M. Wilson, Gwilym Owen, Mervyn Williams,
Herbert Worthington and their contemporaries, gives us all
an insight into the past. The poetical license of an artist
cries out to us from the well-constructed lines; Roy Saunders still holds us, comfortable and relaxed as we turn the
pages of his book, in the palm of his hand. "We sing in our

chains like the sea," eager to read the next few lines, unwilling to put the book down.

His writing transcends half a century and is as applicable today as it was when he first put pen to paper. It could as easily have been written on the parched dry fields of California, in the balmy heat of Georgia, on the green fresh fields of Oregon, or on the steep snow-capped mountains of New Zealand. Close your eyes and you can feel the excited heartbeat of all the young dogs in the world as they see sheep for the first time; you can feel the expectation of every handler on every continent as they walk to the handler's post, and you can smell the earthy lanolin-tinged muskiness of woolly sheep as they turn at your feet.

Welcome to the world of *Sheepdog Glory*!

SHEEPDOG GLORY

Reprinted from the original 1956 edition

◆◆

There is a tide in the affairs of men
Which taken at the flood leads on to fortune.

FOR THE sum of twenty-five pounds, I bought a thin, undersized young sheepdog. My neighbours might well have questioned my sanity in making such a deal. He was certainly a strange sight and, to the layman, looked nothing more than a frail black and white mongrel.

But little Toss was no mongrel. He was the scion of a unique line of trials-winning Border Collie champions, with the blood of J. M. Wilson's Cap and Mirk and Moss, and John Kirk's Nell, in his veins.

This is the story of his development and training for his first season at the sheepdog trials.

Since 1946, when I was suddenly swept into this fascinating business, I have owned other Border Collies; but the understanding between any of them and me has never been sufficient in the rigorous conditions of present-day competition. Little Toss, who stood the test of his first year so successfully, has already taught me more about the game than all the others.

Doubtless he would have been still more successful as a two-year-old if my skill and opportunities for training had been greater. Being a master at a Cardiff High School, I am obliged during the winter to confine to

(9)

week-ends my visits to my flock of sheep—yet I have been trying to exploit Toss's talents in competition with the keenest shepherds in the land. The fact that he and I have done so well together during his first year makes me hopeful that I have in Toss a 'star' in the making.

He is, of course, a working dog, and *Sheepdog Glory* covers the shepherd's year from one September to the next, as well as the trials.

Toss is my constant companion throughout the winter months on all visits to my flock for inspection, safeguarding against predatory animals, rescue from snowdrifts, dealing with straying, caring for lambs and much else besides. These tasks form part of a trial sheepdog's normal background education, which also includes getting used to long car journeys, meeting strangers and doing as much hill work as possible on a variety of courses. Toss, in addition, has even had to appear on the stage!

Then comes the summer, with its thrills and frustrations, triumphs and disappointments, on the trials field. As the shepherd's working year is spent with his dog, so his holiday too revolves round the sport of his dog's training in competition with his rivals and their dogs.

British agriculture is becoming highly mechanised, but even when nearly every part of the farm is worked by machinery, the age-old skill of the shepherd's dog will still be needed to gather in the harvest of the hills.

Introduction

Without the sheepdog's help, control of mountain flocks would be impossible and the 'industry' of mutton production would cease to be.

The sheepdog trial, by-product in sport of this vital industry, may well be classed as the world's cleanest and cleverest animal sport. It is free from bloodshed, cruelty or discomfort for either dog or sheep, completely unmarred by connections with doping or gambling, yet it has the full excitement inherent in the most difficult of the pastoral arts.

Moreover, as a sport it is remarkable what a fascination it exercises on the public even of the big towns and cities—who for the most part have very little idea of practical sheep-farming. When trials are held, busy workers who 'just look in' after lunch on a Saturday may often still be found there at tea-time, completely enthralled by this unique spectacle of animal-man co-operation.

The trials held in Hyde Park, London, where only the cream of handlers are chosen by the International Sheepdog Society in collaboration with the sponsors (the *Daily Express*), have provided a wonderful opportunity for Londoners to see what a Border Collie can do. Press reports for Hyde Park trials speak of 200,000 spectators—nearly half a million townsmen's eyes held spellbound by the movements of a few little dogs from the mountains. Nor are they wrong to be thus spellbound, for when the British Border Collie is working

(11)

competently in the 'National Style', he is on a level of percipience and sensitivity unsurpassed in the whole realm of the animal kingdom.

CHAPTER I

The Son of a Champion

'I've got a Moss puppy just down from Scotland,' announced Harold Hawken, as I entered the yard of his mixed farm, at the edge of one of Cardiff's ever-growing housing estates. I was not much of a dog-buyer, but he knew that I watched with interest the performances of the young sheepdogs which were always passing through his hands on the way to customers. This time he stirred my interest more even than usual, for Moss was my favourite out of all the famous sheepdogs worked by J. M. Wilson of Scotland in the international championships.

A barn-door opened, and out came a pair of youngsters, lively and high-spirited although one was in poor condition. There was no need to ask which was the son of the great Moss. The thinner one had the makings of a beautiful animal, though disguised by the faded and tangled hair which hung about him.

As soon as they saw me they began prancing around, subjecting me to a plentiful mud-spray. After this we

left the yard and climbed the hill outside, making for a
gate which hung between two sycamores. Exhilarated
by their freedom, the two dogs continued their play,
which became increasingly fast and furious. Some distance from the gate, however, the Moss pup's playful-
ness subsided, and he seemed to lose all interest in his
companion's game. Beyond the sycamores and the gate
he could sense something else to which his whole
being, so young, puppyish and completely untrained,
was violently reacting.

Before we reached the gate, the transformation had
become complete. Though only six months old, the
thin, untidy little creature seemed to be no longer a
mere pup. His head and tail had dropped into the
correct positions for an experienced championship
trials dog. His ears were cocked forward, his jaws were
set. For the rest of the distance to the gate he stalked
like a cat in this fashion—until he saw a bunch of sheep
grazing in the middle of the field, when a wonderful
thing happened.

To retrieve sheep to his master, a good sheepdog
must reach the opposite side of the flock as unobtru-
sively as possible. If he were to run straight from the
shepherd, so that the sheep saw him approach, they
would at once run in the opposite direction. Even if
the dog overtook them before they broke right away
they would swing jostling and circling in panic, with
possible tragic results among pregnant ewes. The dog

must go out on a wide casting run so as to come round gently behind the sheep and retrieve them at a speed dictated by his master's whistles.

For human beings such a process of reasoning is very obvious and elementary, but I still marvel at the way this phenomenon of the cast, which farmers and shepherds take for granted, comes to the good sheepdog through an instinctive wisdom, beyond our measuring, stimulated by the sight of sheep. The good dog has inherited this instinct, while the dog which has not inherited it can never be trained to it. In the case of this Moss puppy, his reactions were an extraordinary example of the instinct in all its beauty, swiftness and spontaneity.

After spotting the sheep, he paused for about as long as it takes a thrown ball to pause at the top of its upward flight before it starts to fall. Then, as though his way were barred by an obstacle which only he could see, he darted off to the right. His shortest course to the sheep had indeed been barred—by that same invisible barrier which prevents the young cuckoo from flying northwards in the autumn.

In a wide, easy and flawless arc, the little dog ran out, and 'lifted' the sheep from beyond. Then they quietly trotted down the field to where we stood in amazement beneath the wind-blown sycamores.

'Full marks for the "outrun", full marks for the "lift", and full marks for the "return"—twenty-five out of twenty-five,' muttered the prospective seller at my side.

We stood at six o'clock, and beyond the sheep, exactly at twelve o'clock, crouched this miniature model of a champion trials Border Collie, his eyes blazing from their hairless rims where recent illness had left its mark. He lay tense, ready to intercept the slightest move of sheep to left or right with an instantaneous reflex action. Whichever way we moved to enable the sheep to regain their freedom, their path was always blocked by the unerring untrained pup with the eyes of a panther. So obsessed was he with his responsibility to keep the flock under control that he never even heard our calls to get him away. He was in a way as hypnotised by the ewes as they were by him— and the mutual hypnosis brought the movements of both parties to a complete standstill.

Our attempts to catch him scattered the flock, which of course excited him to vigorous measures for repairing the 'damage'. To him the woolly pattern was continually disintegrating, while every fibre of his being was urging him to keep it intact. The more we split the flock in our efforts to catch him, the more he circled, enveloping and gathering up the loose ends, to unite once more the bleating, blithering mass of mutton.

At last I managed to grab him, and when my hands closed on his neck and back, I felt how excited the little creature had become. He writhed to regain his freedom and the chance to gather once more, but we led him away.

'He'll take a bit of cooling down, Harold,' I gasped as we returned to the farm. 'He's certainly not everybody's dog.' My friend looked at me with a knowing smile, which seemed to say: 'But he's what you've been waiting for.'

The two youngsters had meanwhile resumed their play, and it was only now I realised that a second pup had been with us all the time.

I left the farm and returned home excited but doubtful. I guessed that Harold would have set a good price on the dog, if I had asked him, and I had already found trials an expensive game to follow. I had tried many dogs of varying calibre which had failed to make the grade, and had sold them for less than their cost. For a would-be trialist there were also stiff entry fees, not to mention long car journeys, with petrol at four and something a gallon. But the bug had bitten deep and I was not giving up yet: competition in South Wales was as fierce as anywhere in the British Isles, and I was out to get somewhere whatever the odds.

Would this little highland firebrand turn out to be the dog I sought? That was the question which called for long and earnest consideration. Would he suit me, and what was equally important, would I suit him?

I already had two dogs, one of which had shown

B

good promise at his first season but less at the second, and our partnership was slowly but surely breaking down. That mutual understanding, the essential ingredient in any partnership, had in some unaccountable way gone out of our lives, and 'divorce' was imminent. The other dog, though equally well bred, showed little promise of ever developing into any sort of a trials performer, and I was expecting to have to separate from him too.

The average dog-lover might be shocked at what sounds like a complete absence of sentiment existing between most trial men and their dogs; but the fact is that there is a realistic appraisal of 'compatibility', perhaps more important than in any other man-animal partnership, and without this bond, man and dog will be useless to each other. One type of handler will always have the cool, quiet dog, without much style. Another type will favour the fast, fiery, strong-eyed, stylish creature, and enjoy the long battle to train and bend and break the dog to his needs. All preliminary training must be conducted on the same lines as in the public competitions. The same steady insistent commands must be used over a long period of the dog's early life. After as much as two years of incessant handling, and the experience provided by a further year or two of age, he may then begin to enter the lists in competition with champions: the Border Collie is at his best between the ages of four and seven.

The Son of a Champion

Much thought, in fact, is called for by the trials enthusiast considering buying a new dog, and his state of mind is not so far removed from that of people about to adopt a child. I had to admit to myself, however, as I drove home through the Cardiff traffic, that my heart had been captivated by that splendid little wraith of a dog, with his swift and lovely turns and his evident 'one-track' mind: here was an animal who could at least share my enthusiasm! Then, when I reached home, a walk round the sheep only served to fan the flames of my desire to become his owner. His name was Toss: Toss, son of Moss—it sounded promising.

The following evening found me back at Harold's farm, encouraging myself to take the gamble with the aid of a well-worn fragment from *Julius Caesar*:

> *There is a tide in the affairs of men*
> *Which taken at the flood, leads on to fortune.*

Of men *and* dogs, I said to myself.

'Come on in, Roy, D.L. is here.' This greeting gave me a shock, for D. L. Evans was one of the shrewdest judges of sheepdog quality in South Wales, and I wondered tensely whether he had got in before me. But no, he was on a flying visit connected with other business, and to my relief he had soon departed—without the dangerous temptation of seeing the dogs.

After that we agreed on a price of £25 with a

minimum of bargaining. (Prices range from £6 or £8 for a six-weeks-old pup to £100 or £150 for a good dog showing great promise in its early trials.) Toss was enthroned on the back seat of my car, and a new era in my life had begun!

At first this product of some highland farmyard looked sadly out of place in the trim suburb of Rhiwbina where I live; I decided to screen him from the view of neighbours and visitors until good food began to tell. And here it might be worth putting in a word or two on feeding, for the leanness of even the healthiest hill sheepdog sometimes leads the townsman to imagine them as kept on a near starvation diet by farmers and shepherds. But they should not be compared with the town pet, who usually does nothing all day for its living. They cover a tremendous running mileage on most days of the week and however scraggy some sheepdogs may look, they are fit as an athlete is fit. As regards Toss's personal diet, a sheep's head boiled in a pressure cooker would make two meals. Occasionally he had—and still has—some horseflesh, herrings, rabbit, raw egg or raw liver—the last a special delicacy. Often enough, when none of these are convenient, he simply has bread and milk or porridge. Chicken bones are *never* given, for they splinter and might cut the dog's intestine. He is fed once a day, the last thing at night, which is the normal practice with sheepdogs.

The Son of a Champion

It was not long before good living began to have its effect. Then the jet hair of a new coat began to spread an ever-widening pattern of shining black down his spine, and the wispy neck developed a full white ruff. Round his eyes the bare circles changed to grey and then to black, as the hair came through to clothe the conjunctiva.

As for his emotional life, an unconditional love for his master was won without delay or difficulty. He began to learn from me the set pattern of basic commands which form the essential training for public trials. In return I learnt from him something of the wisdom of the hills, and felt increasingly a deep happiness and inner satisfaction, to be handling at last the splendid sheepdog I had been seeking for so long.

CHAPTER II

The Border Collie Breed

THE Border Collie is never seen at dog shows, and unlike show dogs he is not to be judged by any physical characteristics. He need not conform to a particular colour, shape or size, length of muzzle or height of shoulder. His coat may be fine, long and glossy, harsh and curly, or very short and sleek; all that matters is his brain, temperament, reactions to work, and the consistency of his performance behind sheep. If he has a cast, a wide gather, a strong eye to single out a required sheep; if he moves freely, never barks, never bites; if he is prepared to take orders, is affectionate towards those he knows, regards his master as a sort of god and the sheep pastures as the equivalent of heaven—then, and only then, can he be called a first-class specimen of his breed.

No man-dictated fashions have governed the Border Collie's bodily proportions; his outline has been modelled by the bleak mountain run, with its gullies, screes, stone walls, wind, rain, snow, and miles of heather, fern and rock. Centuries of running on wide hills have evolved a small lightly built animal with a lithe well co-ordinated frame and a stamina for work mentally and physically beyond anything else on four legs.

Despite the apparent insistence on breeding for working qualities alone, most Border Collies are in fact of a handsome appearance. The homozygous tendencies are very strong, and although greys and tans occasionally crop up, about ninety per cent of these dogs are a smartly proportioned black and white. (There is a picturesque theory explaining this combination by the idea that an all-black dog tends to frighten sheep too much, while an all-white dog, being too like the sheep themselves, has little effect on them.)

If the dog is well-marked in black and white in the right places, and is generally pleasant to look at, it is of course so much the better, but a collie which the layman might find strikingly handsome would look ugly and ridiculous to the shepherd if his head and tail were held high. The dog's 'intelligence quotient' is shown more clearly in the carriage of his tail than by any other physical sign, and it is perhaps a pity that we cannot test a child's I.Q. so simply and with such a degree of accuracy. In any case the plain, mismarked, miscoloured sheepdog, whose breeding is right, can give a stylish performance which is fascinating and beautiful—and will easily surpass the performance of the most splendid-looking dog with less good breeding.

To Mr John Herries McCulloch, the Scottish agricultural scientist, must go the credit for extensive research into Border Collie pedigrees. In his two books, *Sheepdogs and their Masters* and *Border Collie Studies*, he has compiled the proof that all winners of the 'Supreme Championship' can be traced back through their pedigrees, as kept in the Society's stud-books, to a single dog:

A study of the pedigrees of the winning dogs reveals some very interesting and important facts, the first and foremost being that all the winners of the Championship Shield at the International Sheepdog Trials since their commencement in 1906 to the present day belong to the same great family, a family within a breed. From the standpoint of pure genetics it is one of the most interesting families in existence.

Secondly, all these dogs are descendants of Old Hemp, born 1893, died 1901, so to that great dog must go the undisputed title of progenitor of the modern Border Collie.

Thirdly, although the Border Collies of today all belong to this one great family, there is little evidence of deleterious inbreeding.

Through nearly half a century of breeding, the tiny particles of heredity have been transmitted from parent to offspring, maintaining the invincibility of this wonderful family through so many generations.[1]

[1] *Border Collie Studies.*

Potential Champions

Puppies from three bitches with whom Old Hemp was mated started off the lines of breeding in which the supreme champions are all to be found. As a result this country has become the breeding-ground and cradle for good sheepdogs, which are exported from it each year to all parts of the world where sheep are bred.

It was by mere chance that one dog was retained out of a batch of youngsters being sent to America just before the second world war. It probably had too much white for the Americans, and it became the property of Mr J. M. Wilson, mentioned earlier, the greatest of all sheepdog trainers. This dog's name was Cap, and although big trials were suspended during the war so that he never became famous throughout Britain, nevertheless his reputation among breeders is almost a legend. Bitches from all over the country were sent to Cap, the great stud-dog of the war years.

Among his descendants his daughters, remarkably enough, inherited his qualities to a far greater extent than his sons. He was, in fact, predominantly a sire of good bitches, and the sequel is equally curious. For when, after the war, the international championships were held once more, it was the sons of these daughters of Cap who became the great winners and pillars of the breed: GLEN (3940) won in 1946 and 1948.

> MIRK (4438) won in 1950.
>
> HEMP (6860) and PAT (4203) won in 1951.
>
> MOSS (5176)—the father of TOSS—was twice in second place.
>
> SWEEP (3834) took third place.

(The numbers are their registration numbers in the

studbook of the International Sheepdog Society, and are quoted because so many dogs are called by the same name.)

At the Worcester International in 1948, first, second and third places went to Glen, Moss and Sweep respectively—all sons of John Kirk's Nell (3514) who was a daughter of Cap. Three sons from the same mother, winning the first three places at the final stage of the supreme championship, was a record never before equalled. It remained to be seen what share in the inheritance of greatness had been handed down to Toss, whose father was Moss.

The tests in the National Style of sheepdog working (the usual and most important style) constitute a difficult set of exercises specially designed to reflect (as far as can be made possible on the trials field) the situations encountered during the dog's daily routine work on the hills, and to demonstrate the specialised faculties of this particular branch of the sheepdog breed. For it is no exaggeration to claim that among all types of sheepdog only the Border Collie can be taught to accomplish these tasks.

Before 1905, when the International Sheepdog Society was formed, many individual trials were staged as a result of those held in the first three centres of 'trialing'—at Bala, Garth, and Groeswen, all in Wales. So it is from my home country that the popularity of the sport has spread all over the world, wherever hard shepherding is practised. (Trials are held today in sheep-farming regions of South and East Africa, Australia and New Zealand, as well as in various parts of America, to which many of our good dogs are exported.)

James Reid, an Airdrie solicitor, was one of the men who evolved the ideas behind the National Style tests, and also one of the chief founders of the International Sheepdog Society (he acted as Hon. Secretary, Treasurer and Keeper of the studbook till 1946 when he retired, to be succeeded by T. H. Halsall of South-port). Every year since the Society's formation (except for war years) it has held an international competition for picked men and dogs from England, Scotland and Wales—in each of the three countries alternately; and all who work good sheepdogs cherish the ambition of qualifying to compete at the International in the hope of winning the Society's supreme award, 'The Blue Ribband of the Heather'. Only pedigree dogs are eligible to enter, and they have to be registered in the studbook.

In the National Style of working each competitor uses five sheep, one of which is marked with a red ribbon tied round its neck. The dog has a long outrun to gather these sheep and retrieve them to his master in a straight line, passing at one point between two poles or hurdles set in the middle of the field. They have to be brought to the shepherd's right-hand side, turned slowly round him and driven away again in a straight line, to pass eventually between another pair of hurdles well over to the left. All this time the shepherd may not move from the post from which the dog was started. The sheep must then be driven across the field to pass between another pair of hurdles well over to the right, marking the corner of the triangular course. They are then returned to the shepherd once more.

At this stage the shepherd is allowed to move into a sawdust ring where two of the four unmarked sheep have to be separated by the dog. Here the shepherd can for the first time give a little practical assistance, by forming an opening for the dog to come in and shed off (or part) the required two sheep.

The five are then united again and taken to a square pen composed of four hurdles, one of which forms the gate; the sheep have to be driven into this tiny pen, after which the handler closes the gate. Finally the five sheep are returned to the ring, and the sheep with the red ribbon has to be singled out for 'wearing' by the dog. 'Wearing' consists of a display by the dog that it has enough 'threat' in its manner to turn the marked sheep away from its fellows, to the satisfaction of the judges, without any show of violence.

Throughout this complicated set of tests the only assistance given by the man is to help to hold the sheep inside the ring and indicate the ones to be separated;

at the pen he merely holds the gate open and closes it when they are all inside.

Usually there are two judges seated at a table or in a small tent or car, and theirs is the unenviable task of taking off the points when sheep go out of line in the drives or miss the hurdles, for second attempts at shedding, allowing sheep to run round the pen, or failing to single properly.

As with many other sports, the 'trialists' have a picturesque special vocabulary, including such terms as the casting outrun, the lift, the fetch, the incoming and outgoing flakes, the off flakes, the shedding, penning, singling, and wearing.

Orders are often whistled, but verbal commands—such as the universal flanking orders to left or right ('come by' and 'away to me', respectively)—are seldom varied. This makes it easier, when a dog is bought or sold, for him to understand quickly the orders of his new master. On the same principle, when a Scottish-trained dog comes to Wales, his new handler must put on a Scottish accent, and keep it up for some time afterwards. A dog trained in Welsh (as many are) would cause some difficulties to a Scottish or English buyer.

Many dogs in Wales take their orders in both English and Welsh. Stanley Jones, a coal miner from the Neath Valley who is also a gifted sheepdog trainer, when he has lost enough points to be out of the running for a prize, will keep the crowd in fits of laughter by giving orders alternately in both languages, all of which the dog obeys.

Sheepdog names vary little: among the commonest are Lark, Glen, Drift, Lass, Craig, Cap, Nell, Sweep, Taff, Jaff, Chip, Moss, Rob, Fan, Scott. All must be simple, so that they are suitable for constant use throughout the day; the ostentatious high-sounding names of the dog show find no place in the shepherd's kennel. Imagine a hill-man cupping his hands about his mouth and shouting to his two dogs working a flock on the opposite mountain—'That'll do there, Golden Ponsonby of Princetown'—'Come on up, Burlington Blockbuster of Bloomsbury.'

Sheepdog names are as old as the calling itself, and the first primitive pastoralist of pre-history who herded stock and taught a dog to help him, probably called it with a monosyllabic grunt. So may these short and lovely names never change, but pass on from generation to generation of dogs and men as long as the hills and the breed and the calling last.

CHAPTER III

OCTOBER–NOVEMBER

Sheepdog on the Stage

DURING the winter I am frequently asked to give lectures, mainly on natural history, both for the Extra-Mural department of Cardiff University College and for such groups as Scouts, Women's Institutes, old-age pensioners, young farmers' clubs and so on. The winter after I had bought Toss brought its usual crop of engagements. I had always especially enjoyed giving talks on sheepdogs with the help of miniature lantern slides and blackboard sketches, and one evening I decided to take young Toss along to help demonstrate certain points. He had, of course, been working with me for some months, and was shaping very well. The experience with crowds would be useful to him, and I was sure that the presence of a dog would add to the popularity of a subject which always seemed to go down particularly well.

To me the experiment seemed, at first, only partly successful. Toss demonstrated the flanking moves, the stop and the steady approach, but his performance, though adequate, was rather mechanical, like the drill of a performing Alsatian; his sense of style could not be roused without the all-important stimulus of sheep. The audience, however, was delighted and it was no use trying to convince them how different it would have been if they had seen him at work on real live-stock.

I drove home thinking hard: to my knowledge no one had ever had the temerity to work a dog with sheep on a lighted stage. The idea, in fact, was obviously absurd, but it occurred to me that one might use a substitute—why not ducks?

The following week I was due to address the members of Cardiff's Roath Park Congregational Church. I rang up the Rev. Mr Salmon who had engaged me, and asked him if it would be possible to demonstrate the dog's manœuvres using live ducks on the stage. He readily agreed, so there was no turning back: the experiment must be tried.

Next day I borrowed three ducks and started rehearsing. They happened to be Cross-Muscovy ducks and were supposed to be good fliers; for all I knew, they might have taken wing for a trip round the audience.

I made a little portable pen, and it was a simple matter to manœuvre them into it on the lawn. The ducks learnt this 'trick' very easily, and as Toss came round with his familiar crouch and intense glare, they

(33)   c

would make for the sanctuary of the pen. I did not want to make it look too easy, however, so when this had been done a few times I refrained from further practice.

The announcement of our performance was made from the pulpit the Sunday before the show, and the hall was crowded. After the usual lecture and projection of slides, I introduced my partner, who had until that point been kept in the background.

Our performance began with Toss jumping on to the table as I tapped it and giving me his paw. In the midst of the applause which greeted this simple move there came unusual sounds, the hysterical quacking of my ducks from their basket backstage. I gave the signal to my helper to bring them on, and the three bewildered birds appeared. The pen was put up and Toss crouched ready.

Gone was the goofy expression and wagging tail. Every line of him had passed through a complete transformation. Head down, mouth set, eyes blazing, ears cocked forward and body tensed, he waited. The three ducks bunched with heads erect, looking hopelessly in different directions. I inched the dog forward slightly, the ducks moved towards the pen, it was obvious to me that they could be 'waddled in' with ease. Amidst an amazed silence from the audience, they were soon penned and the gate shut. It was over all too soon, I felt, but everyone was happy except the ducks. Their unhappiness, it is true, produced certain physical results irrelevant to the main action, which I decided would have to be the caretaker's pigeon on the following morning.

Toss enjoyed giving these performances. When he stood before an applauding audience, bathed, groomed and faintly self-conscious, I always felt that he looked particularly pleased with himself and was reacting to the limelight (as any sensitive dog is bound to react) in a way that was only animal, as one might say 'only human'. His evident pride combined with the 'intelligence' of his performance would usually make an audience overestimate his 'human' characteristics. Dogs, however, are not 'human' and should not be judged by human standards. Whatever feats the future Border Collie may perform as the breed evolves, canine psychology will remain very different from ours and it will always be a mistake to expect too much from a dog's 'intelligence', in the strict sense of the word. I have found that training dogs is not unlike a University Honours graduate teaching a class of small boys: his teaching will only become effective when he understands how little they know about the subject on which he knows so much. But the gulf between man and dog does not, to my mind, make any less wonderful the manifestations of a dog's 'instinctive understanding'— and in any case this is not the sort of thing which it is easy to get across to an audience.

(35)

Sheepdog Glory

At one point in the training of Toss I introduced the supersonic whistle, its note having a frequency too high for detection by human ears. This high-pitched note was quite inaudible to me when I blew, yet Toss would hear it and stop when running a hundred yards away. I soon saw that some extra amusement with audiences could be derived from this.

I would go to the back of the hall, leaving Toss sitting on the stage, then explain to him that I wanted him to cross over to the top step and sit down. The little dog, of course, understood nothing of what I was saying, but the well-known command to flank in that direction would start him off towards the steps, on reaching which he would appear to freeze as though he had suddenly remembered my order. No one, of course, heard the whistle which stopped him, and I would often go on with this trick, varying it with the geography of the stage.

Sometimes I would reveal my secret, but this usually served to astound people even more. For some reason they found it difficult to imagine that a dog can hear something which a human being cannot. Yet it is only a matter of anatomical difference, and most people accept as obvious that dogs have much more acute powers of smell than we have; so why should their hearing organs not be more sensitive as well?

We are far superior to the dog, however, in eyesight—although we could not compete, for instance, with the high-flying carrion vultures, whose appetites and lives depend on exceptional distance vision. Most sheepdogs I have trained have had poor sight compared with human beings and were quite unable to recognise sheep a long distance away. Even to the rule of canine shortsightedness, however, Toss seemed to be the exception.

When we came to take part in trials he would sit awaiting his turn, watching every move in the work of his rivals. At the end of the run, when the next competitor moved out to his place, Toss would sit up and watch the distant point where the sheep were being released, sometimes as far away as three fields. The course director would wave his flag, and with the first move of the distant pen men, Toss would prick up his ears and watch with fresh enthusiasm. His sight was almost as keen as his other senses, and very little escaped their combined perception.

CHAPTER IV

A Matter of Training

WHATEVER orders are given to the working collie, they must be clearly understood and obedience must be insisted on. Toss had to be firmly disciplined in the early days. Petting was forbidden at all times except when a sequence of moves had been well conducted; then, and only then, was he given a pat and a word of approval, At the start of his career, too much petting would have ruined him—and at all times the trialist's affection for his dog must be devoid of sentimentality. Our admiration for them rests entirely on what they can do, and for us they are not 'pets' in the ordinary sense.

It is, of course, no use merely asking a young dog to do something and expecting obedience. The verbal command means nothing when first given unless accompanied by a clear demonstration of what is wanted. The action or gesture must go with the word until the association of action and word stimulates the required reflex movement. Very soon the sound of the word is enough and the action is no longer needed.

Some take longer than others to learn, and naturally no two are alike, just as no two trainers are alike.

A Matter of Training

Methods vary in every case, but it is the easy way out
to blame a dog when he fails to obey an order; the fact
is that he has never been made to understand clearly
what is required.

There is one golden rule in teaching the Border
Collie all the complicated manœuvres needed for competition in the National style: never use the stick.
Those who refuse to obey this rule seem to be crediting
the dog with an understanding of words equal to that
of a human being, so that his repeated refusals to obey
are treated as signs of extreme stupidity or wilfulness
requiring a thrashing in punishment. Such handlers
are rare, but when they compete in trials they are all
too conspicuous and the nervous dog gets his own
back by giving his master away. Being an extremely
sensitive animal, the Border Collie who has once been
thrashed with a stick will always continue to advertise
this in his behaviour. In fact, in the words of Wyndham
Harris, winner of the Welsh National in 1950 and a
well-known trials judge: 'When you go to train a
young dog, leave the stick at home.'

As an example of the dangers of using the stick, I
recall the occasion at the Welsh National Championships at Swansea when Herbert Worthington's Moss,
several times winner of the Shepherd's trophy at the
International Society's trials, was set upon by Lad,
owned by B. H. Davies of Talgarth. A friend raised his
stick to separate the fighting dogs, but Herbert, al-

though his valuable dog was having the worst of it, snatched the stick away from his friend, and dashed in to separate them with his bare hands. He would not even allow his dog to see his attacker being touched by the stick. For the stick plays too great a part in shedding and singling, when the dog has to come in beneath the raised stick to separate the required sheep, which he would hesitate to do had he once felt its sting. It should always be regarded as an important tool, essential to the loved work of shepherding, and never as an instrument of punishment.

How much praise should be given to a sheepdog for good work? Some experts hold that a dog may become headstrong if told he is good, and start thinking he is better than he is. For the keen sheepdog's instinct, the advocates of this theory explain with justice, is to do the job his own way, whereas to satisfy his owner's requirements he must do it in another way. His eager canine impulses can only be controlled by trained orders, and he must be held in check under firm command. A sudden softening in the voice of whoever is commanding can be mistaken for weakness; he may immediately feel free to move into a position of his own choosing, and control has gone.

On the other side, surely no dog will go on indefinitely giving devoted service if praise is withheld when praise is due. It is my view, therefore, that when a sheepdog, who understands so little of our complicated speech, has carried out a good move, he should never be left in doubt that he has done well. That is the best way for his master to make known to him what is wanted in the future—and how a sheepdog loves to please his master! There is no parallel to the joy in a

sheepdog's eyes when he has done a job well and receives the simple reward of a clap on the flanks and the magic words: 'Good dog!'

The correct attitude for the shepherd, then, is a combination of firmness, dignity, even a certain reserve, with kindness and unlimited patience: the better you keep your temper, the more your own calm will be imparted to the dog, the better your chance of winning that silent service and devotion which is beyond ordinary understanding.

A wonderful story of a dog's devotion to duty comes from the Peebles district of Scotland. A certain dealer owned a clever little Border Collie bitch; when he bought in a flock of sheep at one of the markets where he traded he would usually send the flock home under the care of his dog, so that he had his hands free for other matters. The flock would be well on their way home by the time he got back, and sometimes were there before him.

One night the new sheep failed to arrive, and on the following morning there was still no sign of them or the dog. Such a thing had never happened before; the dealer grew anxious, and mounting his pony made off over the hills in the direction from which the sheep were expected.

At last he met them coming slowly home, the sheepdog driving from behind, and carrying what appeared to be a rabbit. Thinking that she had spent the night rabbiting, he was about to reprimand her, but on coming closer he could see that she was carrying a newly born sheepdog pup.

At some point on the journey the little bitch had been obliged to relinquish her great responsibility for an even greater one. After giving birth to her litter, she had picked one of them up and carried on with her job. (A full-time shepherd, of course, would never rely on one dog only, particularly a bitch; when in season bitches have to be kept in a closed shed.)

The dealer put the puppy into his pocket, and the sheep were taken home. No sooner had they been folded than the mother set off back to her litter, and eventually returned home with a second pup. Then she went back again for a third, and then a fourth, but the last pup was dead, having been exposed for too long.

It is fascinating to imagine the dog struggling on behind her charges until, with the last of the pains, she had to crawl into the bracken to make her bed. How long did she spend in licking and suckling her babies, before making her great decision to go on, the call of duty superseding even the anxieties of motherhood?

Of such a mould is the Border Collie fashioned.

◆◆◆

CHAPTER V

DECEMBER

◆◆◆

Foot-and-Mouth on the Next Farm

IT WAS nearly midnight, the December wind was howling in the chimney, and the fire was hard to leave. Toss suddenly got up, and stood tense, listening, while a faint growl rose in his throat. Only an emergency could make him growl, and I thought it must be a burglar. Then came the sound of a confident tread, at which his tension subsided, and so did mine.

It was the policeman. 'Sorry to tell you, Mr Saunders, but foot-and-mouth has been confirmed at Emrys Bassett's place, Rhiwbina Hill Farm. No animals must be moved until the ban is lifted.'

I returned miserably to the fire. Life is so short that I usually grudge the few hours of sleep; but now there was no pleasure in staying awake and I went to bed—stunned by the news and the consequences it might have for me.

My flock at the time of the outbreak was in two lots. The breeding ewes were on Cefn Carnau hill, an area of some thirty acres of grazing land, a mile or so from

the house but with only a quarter of a mile of woodlands between them and the outbreak. The other half,
a flock of bought-in lambs, were grazing on some
fields adjoining the infected farm.

When foot-and-mouth strikes, there is no warning.
One minute you have all your stock to worry about,
and the next—you needn't worry about them any
more, for vets and police and ministry officials and
workmen will descend upon you to kill all the cloven-
hoofed stock and burn the infected carcases.

At first light on the following morning I carried out
a quick inspection, Toss of course being left at home.
The lambs were in fine condition, as indeed were
twenty or so young cattle owned by Mr Bassett which
grazed in the next field beyond the forbidden boundary. As I learnt later in the day, he had reported the
contracting of the disease by one of his pigs, the vets
had confirmed it, and so all his livestock would have
to be killed at once. He would, of course, be com-
pensated financially for his losses, but this is little con-
solation to a farmer who has to start again from scratch
with new stock.

I went off to school as if nothing had happened, but
everyone was talking about Emrys' misfortune, usually
predicting that it would be my turn next; and every
time a prefect came towards me, I expected him to tell
me of a 'phone call from the foot-and-mouth centre.
Late in the afternoon I *was* called to the telephone, but

it was only Harold Hawken talking quite without his usual confident assurance. Much of his life's work had been bound up with the Ministry of Food and he had a great respect for the vets and officials concerned. He advised me to keep off the land and certainly, at all costs, to keep the valuable Toss clear of any contact and suspicion.

Meanwhile the slaughter at Emrys's place proceeded: eighty splendid breeding ewes and forty-eight cattle, including his fine milking herd, went down Rhiwbina Hill for the last time. Only one pig had shown the symptoms, yet all the animals, which were probably quite healthy, had to pay the penalty.

On my way home I called at the police station to see if they knew anything about the position of my own stock, but they could tell me nothing. I waited a couple of days in horrible anxiety, and at last on Friday the call came through: 'Barry Foot-and-mouth Centre speaking.' Now for it, I thought. I was informed that the lambs would be inspected on the following morning at ten o'clock and my presence during the test was required.

Next morning was as mild and calm as June. The naked ash trees were etched against the dull red glow in the eastern sky; 'Red sky at morning, shepherd's warning.' It is strange how, when something preys heavily on the mind, one is at the mercy of all manner of superstitions and omens. Then a dark fox appeared

and calmly loped away, pausing in the centre of the
field to look back at me. I saw little beauty in his easy
grace that morning, and remained unmoved by the
tameness which gave me time to watch him. I thought
of him not as a killer of lambs or the animal so many
folk love to hunt, but as the perfect carrier of foot-añd-
mouth virus from one farm to another.

The light increased and skeins of herring gulls flew
calmly inland from their night roosts on Steepholm
island or the Channel cliffs. I watched them passing
over with easy wing-beats in the tranquil splendour of
the winter's dawn, until suddenly I thought of them
too as carriers of the plague. I felt a furious resentment
against all the other potential carriers—peewits, crows,
starlings, badgers and the rest—and went up alone to
gather my suspect lambs for scrutiny by the vets.

They were quiet enough, and I had to drive them
hard to get them down. They fanned out on a broad
front with a determined leader at the two extreme ends
of the line, each wanting to lead his fellows in different
directions. My job would have been so easy with a
swift and agile sheepdog. As I plodded from one end
of the line to the other, to and fro, time after time, I
realised fully how much I was missing the faithful Toss.
At last I reached the shelter of the old barn. They filed
in, I slammed the door on them, and went home for a
second breakfast.

I returned at ten o'clock and soon afterwards a big

car came up the lane. Two vets got out of the car, put on black rubber mackintoshes, rubber trousers and Wellingtons, washed themselves down with dettol, and then examined all the lambs' feet. A touch of footrot in two of them held their attention for a time, but they were soon declared fit. So far I was safe.

I changed my boots and set off by car to Cefn Carnau hill. On the way I passed the entrance to the forbidden farm, and saw the signs which accompany an outbreak of foot-and-mouth: notices on either side of the gate, a row of green Agricultural Committee vans, several mud-splashed cars, a County Council roadman's shelter with a lighted brazier in front which guarded the entrance to the farm day and night. A strange policeman on duty looked at me suspiciously as I passed by. Emrys and his family were prisoners in their own home; only officials and decontamination squads could pass in and out.

At the high corner where the road bends into the woodlands leading to my place, I stopped to look back. Not a living thing moved, a strange depressing silence brooded over the sunlit meadows where a splendid herd and a beautiful flock had grazed some days before. A big mobile crane towered above the buildings, and the smoke from a smouldering fire drifted sadly across the silent scene.

My ewes were grazing quietly on the five-acre field below the beeches, oblivious of the fate which had

Foot-and-Mouth on the Next Farm

D

come so close. Old ginger, grey-face and tan-face looked up from their grazing and seemed to be watching me enquiringly as I walked between them. To my amazement some of them came towards me, evidently expecting something. Sheep have a phenomenal associative memory. The only time they ever see me without a dog is during the month before lambing starts, when a ration of ewe-cake is distributed, and now they 'deduced' that because I had appeared without Toss, the time for cake had come again. Although nearly a year had passed since I had been there without a dog and given them their dearly-loved ration, seeing me alone reawakened the memory—for the ewes which came up to me were the ones which loved sheep-cake most.

There were no signs of the disease having reached them, but I nailed a notice on the gate where the public footpath entered the field, requesting the public not to use the footpath during the critical time which lay ahead. The smoke from the burning on Rhiwbina Hill crept slowly up the Nofydd valley, but I returned home feeling easier—and with my fingers tightly crossed.

As it happened, my luck held, and my flock was spared.

◆◆

CHAPTER VI

JANUARY

◆◆

Digging Sheep out of the Snow

IT WAS a Saturday night in January, a bitter wind from the east whined dismally about the house, and I left the fire reluctantly to take Toss for a short walk. Apart from the hissing of the wind in the hedge, everything was quiet: I felt the lurking threat of snow.

After our walk I put Toss back into his shed and returned to the fire in time for the weather forecast, to learn that roads in the north had been blocked by snow drifts. The last word was a grim one for the shepherd: ordinary snow means little to strong sheep, but drifting snow is a different proposition. Ewes shelter in the lee of hedgebanks, and the wind-blown snow, caught in the lee eddy, piles in upon them. All night they sleep snugly, sheltered from the wind, breathing through a hole formed by their warm breath. But in the morning they are held prisoner by six feet of piled-up snow.

When I woke next morning my fears were confirmed. The world had changed colour, the wind was

howling, and fine dry snow was blowing west before
the gale. I could see ahead of me a Sunday of unremitting search and toil. I put on my oldest clothes and
Wellingtons, had a good breakfast, packed some food
for the day, with a flask of brandy and a thermos of
hot milk in case of need, for an exhausted sheep will
respond to a drench of brandy. I also took my six-foot
shepherd's crook, normally kept for the more showy
trials of August. But this was the real thing, and the
crook would be needed now to probe the drifts, feeling
for buried sheep.

Toss came out into the stinging wind, blinking
violently—he had never seen snow before—and we
set off up the road. After a few hundred yards I turned
back, for my Wellingtons were full of snow, and I
decided to change them for boots and puttees.

When younger I had revelled in winter sports, and
my climb that morning soon brought its rewarding
warmth as I toiled upwards in the deepening snow of
the Wenallt road. But my old love of snow had given
place to dread and hatred, and this element, which I
had travelled to Switzerland to enjoy, had now become
a deadly enemy to be fought and overcome.

As I climbed, the wind increased, and the same fine
dry snow was piled deeper in the lee of the hedges on
my right. In places the drifts were already above eye
level, built up and twisted into fantastic hillocks over-
hung by cornices and cut by gullies. It was astonishing

that this twisted, ridged and frozen desert of white could have been fed by the clouds and carved out by the howling wind in one night.

Thoroughly warmed by now, and stimulated by a sense of adventure, I could almost have exulted in the savage beauty of that morning, but the desperate shepherd in me was too strong for any such poetic feelings. My fifty animals, worth £8 a piece, were still a mile away, and they might all be buried.

After floundering over and through more drifts between the hedges of the narrow road, I decided to make for the open fields, where the going was obviously easier, the grass in some places being quite exposed.

At last I reached the Wenallt top, from where normally I can look across to my fields on the other side of the valley; but today the wind and snow made staring impossible. I plunged on down the slope and came at last to the Wenallt farm, where Councillor Watson's bailiff was feeding the cattle. Through his binoculars I tried to count my sheep, but the wind kept whipping the tears into my eyes, and counting was difficult. At last I was satisfied that forty-two were visible, so my hopes began to rise.

I borrowed a spade, and after a mug of hot sweet tea and a cigarette I plodded on into the blizzard. Young Toss was already tired after his continual plunging through the drifts, and at last it dawned on him that if he kept in behind me, somewhat like King Wenceslas' page, the going would be easier. In this way we reached the brook and started climbing again through the wood and out on to the wind-swept ploughland, through the old deserted farm. At last we came to my sloping six-acre field, which the wind had blown bare of snow in places. The sheep were nuzzling in the shallow places for a picking to satisfy their desperate hunger. They lifted their heads as I climbed the gate, a blob of snow on the nose of each ewe adding to the look of bewilderment on their faces. I counted them, and found there were forty-four—leaving six still to be accounted for.

All but the tops of the hedges were hidden by the snow. Needing a rest badly, I sat on top of the five-bar gate, the topmost bar being the only one left in sight, and wondered where to begin. I tried to imagine where I would have lain for the night had I been a sheep. The hedge nearest the east suggested itself. There the drifts lay deepest, in extraordinary humps and grottoes and weird promontories, like miniature cliffs overhanging a white and frozen sea.

I started at one end, using my six-foot crook to probe the snow at intervals of about two feet. Sometimes I soon felt the ground, at others my hand and arm had to follow the stick in right up to the armpit. A sheep might be buried beyond, untouched by my ferrule, and it would take hours to probe the hundred and fifty yards of the hedge. Not that I would have grudged the long hours of hard digging if I could only find the spot to begin. Despite all the snow, the outlook was pretty black!

Toss had recovered his high spirits and seemed to be watching me quizzically. I went on probing till my right hand became too cold, and then changed over to the left. When that became too cold, I transferred to the right again then back to the left—until both hands were so frozen that I could no longer face pushing either of them in again. All the powdery snow going up my arm had melted on my skin, and I was drenched beyond the elbows.

I noticed that Toss had started digging furiously, in one particular place. Thinking he was after a rabbit, I called him harshly away in case he got buried; in any case I did not want him to start taking an interest in rabbits. He stayed with me for a while but soon slipped back again to his digging. There was something about his manner as he went back which sent a surge of hope through me: it was almost as if he were returning, irresistibly, to sheep. I rushed over to him, and now his head was down the hole. He took a long-drawn sniff and then continued scratching furiously at the snow. I dashed for the spade and started digging beside him. My leather jerkin was soon off, my overcoat followed it, then my sports coat. I dug and dug, and Toss made it obvious that we were on to our buried treasure. I probed again with the crook, and

(55)

Digging Sheep out of the Snow

felt at last the soft yielding body of a sheep. At that point I realised that it had stopped snowing and the sky had lightened. I got to work vigorously, and some minutes later felt the spade on wool. I dug round it and heaved the animal out. She was stiff and cramped, but after a few moments she walked unsteadily away towards her mates. I soon dug out another, and then another, until the sixth came struggling from her snowy tomb. A gush of warmth came with her, and the strong smell of sheep.

They had probably been quite warm inside and would have lived for days, perhaps weeks, until the snows melted. Seven weeks is claimed to be the longest period for which a buried sheep can live. When the snow melted, the head of the animal which had survived its ordeal of hunger and cramp would be left exposed—defenceless against the carrion crows which would descend on it, and stab out the eyes and tongue. It is a grisly end.

My Sunday's labour had been well repaid. I watched the freed animals amble away to join the flock in their search for grass. The brandy and hot milk had been brought for them, but I decided they had better remain teetotal; my need seemed greater than theirs.

I untied a bale of hay kept ready in the shed, the feeding rack was filled, and the sheep came running. I left them pulling and munching as I turned for the struggle homewards in the fading light.

That night, when my small boy came for his bed-time story, there was no need to strain imagination's realm. The story was there, ready-made, in that day's saga of the snows, and his eyes grew wider and rounder than usual. As the yarn went on, the doubts and fears and strain which had been mine throughout the day, were reflected on his face. But the flash of joy with which it lit up when he heard of the vital part played by Toss in finding the sheep—that was as rewarding as the toil itself had been.

Some days later came one of the sweetest sounds which a shepherd can hear: the first melancholy drip of melting snow at the edge of the woods and along the hedgerows. To me no dawn chorus of birds can equal the pleasure of hearing that steady beat of moisture falling on to sodden leaves. The grip of frost and snow is broken, and over the grim white hills and fields dun patterns of pasture spread in ever-widening areas, until there remain only thin white glistening crescents of shallow snow to indicate where the deadly drifts had been.

....

CHAPTER VII

FEBRUARY

....

Tommy Jones, Treorchy

DURING the winter it makes a pleasant diversion to visit the homes of rival trialists and watch them at work on their dogs—it is a chance to see champions performing on their own ground, where they always work their best, and also to find out which youngsters are on their way up. For there is a special interest in watching a young sheepdog's development—or indeed in developing him yourself—while he is still eager, sensitive and willing to listen and respond in the way that you want and not in his own way, as so often happens when a dog matures and grows to think more determinedly for himself.

It was a cold Sunday afternoon in February when I set off for the little home of Tommy Jones, Tal y Fedw farm in a small valley near the Rhondda.

Toss of course was with me, as it would have been unthinkable to make such a visit alone; the first question would have been 'Where's your dog?' For an important part of the training consists of working a young dog on a variety of courses and meeting different types of sheep and situations. In addition, of course, it reduces the fear that through working on your own you may have unwittingly developed wrong tactics. If your methods are exposed to a fresh critical eye, mistakes can be pointed out and rectified.

Young dogs must also get used to travelling by car, indeed they must be taught to love it as the prelude to fresh joys of shepherding. Toss, I am sure, regards the car as a vehicle which flies him to paradise, and when I opened the door saying 'In the back, Toss'—he was on the back seat in one excited bound, hungry for the excitements of the trip.

It was only some fifteen miles to Tommy's place, and from the narrow twisting road of the Ynysybwl valley the little farm showed up on the hillside. The winding track led up in a zigzag course across the fields, to end in a fearful hairpin bend before the final incline to the farm. With some relief I came out safely on the level before the front door, to be hailed by Tommy in his working clothes and Wellingtons. We went inside, and were soon talking happily before a roaring fire.

Of all the colourful characters in the game, few have reached the fame of little Tom, which was spread far and wide by the superb nature film, *Sheepdog* (starring him and Scott, his white dog), by bills and banners and posters, and by a great many articles in the press, which called him 'the wonder Shepherd of Wales'. It may be said that at one stage the orthodox world of sheepdog men were a good deal shocked both by the series of amazing performances Tommy gave, and by the publicity they won him.

The conditions of his work were unique, for he was a shepherd employed by the colliery companies, and would go up on the lonely hilltops which separate the deep glens of the coalfield, with his pony and his dogs as his sole companions. Successful shepherding of these bleak tracts of land called for peculiar tactics with his animals—and they succeeded brilliantly because of the remarkable comradeship which grew up between pony, dogs and man. Critics have poured scorn on his 'stunts', but they were all legitimate aids to his lonely and exacting work above the Rhondda. There was no exhibitionism about it, and when he started these 'tricks', he had no thought of future films and press publicity.

It began with the difficulty of having to carry on with other tasks while not neglecting orphaned lambs. Great ravages were caused by dogs worrying the sheep —they still are today—and many ewes died giving birth to their lambs. The lambs were often saved, and would then have to be bottle-fed until a sheep which had lost its own lamb could be induced to accept the orphan as foster-child.

Carrying milk to these babies took up so much of

Tom's time that he trained a young dog called Scott to take a bottle of milk to them in their walled enclosure a mile from home. Throughout the lambing season there was always some motherless lamb in this enclosure, and time after time the white dog could be seen ascending the slope of the well-worn sheeptrack, to leap the wall and sit while the lamb pulled at the bottle. When it was empty, Scott would return again to the homestead in the valley.

Tom started teaching his dogs other useful tricks. A ewe unable to throw her lamb would need his assistance, and as there was nowhere to tie his pony on the open moor, it seemed quite natural and sensible to train one of the dogs to hold the reins between his jaws. An equally natural outcome of this was to have the dog actually leading the pony. Then again, to help his dogs to sight sheep, Tom trained them to climb on to his shoulders for a more elevated view.

*

It was to Scott the lamb-feeder that Tommy owed the success of his early shepherding days. The bottle-carrying dog was soon noticed, became the talk of the district and then the valley, till eventually he was invited to give a demonstration at Romilly Park, Barry.

This started the ball rolling, and thereafter the strange team of a man, a pony, some sheepdogs and a pet lamb, went from one success to another. He was besieged with requests to put on the show in many parts of the country, and when the Welsh National Sheepdog Trials came to Cardiff, Mr James Reid, the Secretary, sent a telegram to Tommy: 'Come down and give your show.' So Tommy and a friend duly rode off to Cardiff on a motor-bike, two dogs and the pet lamb wedged between them, and milk bottles bulging from their pockets.

Mr Reid put them to a test. The lamb was hidden behind a car at the other end of Sophia Gardens field, the milk bottle was handed to the dog, and he went off in search of the lamb. To the crowd's joy he soon found it and brought it into the open to suck until the bottle was dry.

For several years Tom was a popular figure at Birmingham Floral Fête, where he appeared each year with his dogs and a pet lamb; the bandaged milk bottle was paying a handsome dividend.

Eventually a film company came down to Treorchy, and a picture of Tom, his pony, and the dogs, with yet another pet lamb, was made on the mountains above his home. The full film sequence was made from the pouring of the milk into the bottle, watched by the ever-devoted Scott, through the dog's whole run, finishing with his jumping the wall to sit panting, but still holding on to the bandaged bottle while the lamb sucked. At the Odeon, Leicester Square, the Duke and Duchess of Kent attended the trade show of *Sheepdog*, which went overseas and was the only nature film selected for showing at the World's Fair held in New York.

Tom and his dogs appeared on the stage to support the film, and offers came from Bertram Mills' circus. But then the war came and Tom had less and less time available for teaching his 'wonder dogs', and giving these demonstrations of their work. He settled in a

Scott and the Lamb

(64)

farm of his own in a valley near Treorchy, and today, though his heart is still with sheepdogs, they must take second place to the greater needs of increased milk production.

Scott was no pedigree Border Collie with a long line of champions behind him, but an ordinary Welsh hill dog of no great promise as a youngster. Yet in some unaccountable way he developed 'mentally' to a degree unknown in other dogs. Speaking of him, Tom Jones declares that he was the only dog, out of the hundreds he has owned, who could be said to think for himself as if actually reasoning things out.

★

Tom talked on and on, and the winter afternoon closed in. He was anxious to see young Toss in action and to show me his own two youngsters, so we left the cosy fireside and walked out on to the bleak hills as the lights in the mining valleys came out. In a small walled field we gathered some sheep and watched the paces of our respective dogs. At such times as these no holds are barred and any weaknesses displayed by the animals are freely commented on. This evening, however, Tom was visibly impressed by Toss and declared it in no uncertain terms. The assurance of such an old hand at the game was all that I needed to hear and I returned home with fresh confidence because little Toss had stood the test of Tom's critical eye.

E

CHAPTER VIII

MARCH

The Dreamer on the Skyline

WINTER slowly turned to spring and with the lengthening evening light I was able to make more frequent visits to my flock on Cefn Carnau hill. These visits often had their own interest and excitement. There was always the possibility of a premature birth, a visit from sheep-worrying dogs, or strays coming in from the mountain to help eat up the already close-bitten February grass. Sometimes my own stock would break out in search of a fresh bite on a neighbour's land—which did not add to their owner's popularity. In such cases, Toss was of inestimable value with his sure find, wide gather and gentle return. Every week his prowess developed and the pleasures of training him grew accordingly. Harsh words were always few and far between, and patience, the shepherd's secret weapon, proved increasingly effective.

By March, however, this incidental work was being reduced considerably, since the ewes were heavy with the approach of lambing, and in this month the less they saw of any dog, even a Border Collie, the better. Toss was to come into his own again in April when, one at a time but in quick succession, the ewes start delivering their young.

Meanwhile he needed as much exercise as ever, and he took as much delight as I did in our week-end walks together, sometimes quite unconnected with the flock; though Toss would probably have been still happier if he had been working with sheep, for a dog of his breed it was already much to be away on the hills. As for me, although, of course, I spent a great deal more time in the country than most townsmen can do—more's the pity for them—yet after even the shortest winter I could still seem to myself like one 'too long in city pent'. But now the spring days were here once more; and what days some of them were!

I remember with particular vividness one Saturday in March, which in the sheltered valley seemed deceptively mild, so that Toss and I set off on our long tramp with some degree of freedom from the elements. Yet from the direction of the hills came the roaring of the tempest in the bare trees. I anticipated with relish a wild encounter on my hill-top—where the view on clear days encompasses seven counties.

Between bursts of sunlight there was a hint of rain in the wind, but I kept to my course, and by muddy lanes came at last to the base of the hill where my sheep lived. Down below me, the wooded glen snuggled in sheltered warmth, but far above I could hear the wild song of the west wind, tearing over the skyline with the roar of a night express. The ascent was too sharp for a direct assault, and I took the line of least resistance by crossing diagonally the level contours of the sheep tracks.

It was a rare day of infectious March madness. Cattle careered along the slopes with tails flying, and a brace of hares circled and dodged each other at fantastic speed over one of the high fields. I climbed on gaily, with the wind singing in my ears and roaring in the branches of the trees.

My shadow was with me too, the friend who had kept me company on so many similar hill walks; that young but 'good old' friend for life who sometimes led the way and sometimes lagged behind, but who never tired of my company. He never jibbed at the stiffest climb or set too hard a pace to follow. Toss and I plodded upwards together above the valley and into that sublime atmosphere of detachment from the world which at all times is good for human beings— and perhaps for dogs as well. In every way we were at one with Tennyson's words:

> *On the hills like gods together,*
> *Careless of mankind.*

The west side of the hill, which fell away towards the sun, ran steeply downward. Along this fern-clad slope the forces of the wind-god were gathered and compressed, to be released in almost irresistible power where the beech trees marked the skyline of the hill. Along that line I battled on, leaning well over to maintain a foothold, until at last I stood in triumph on the jagged limestone summit.

I set my feet against some rocks and laughed my heart out at the west wind's efforts to dislodge me. Then, as though taunted to the limit of endurance, he flung his weight against me, tearing at my tangled hair and whipping the tears from my eyes.

I laughed again and shouted back some crazy yell of exultation born of the struggle, as I recalled some lines on the 'Song of the West Wind'.

> *Oh I am the enemy most of might,*
> *The other be whom you please.*
> *Gunner and guns may all be right,*
> *Flags a-flying and armour tight,*
> *But I'm the fellow you've first to fight,*
> *The giant that swings the seas.*

All the while, beyond the Taff gorge and the great Garth mountain in the west, the clouds crept on along the hills and valleys of the mid-Glamorgan coalfield, glowering and threatening. But on my hill the sun kept shining and my spirits were high. To the north the grey glens of the Rhondda intersected in sombre tones, save where the twin arcs of a pair of rainbows cut the gloom. The rounded hump of Mayo mountain, draped about with a skirting of fields and farms, took the eye round to the western valleys of Monmouthshire, and faintly in the distance beyond, to the Brecon Beacon peaks where they touched the passing panoply of cloud.

In the hollow below, the giant ruined fortress of Caerphilly Castle stood sentinel at the gateway to the western valleys of Monmouthshire. But the wandering eye went on to the east, over the Vale of Rhumney to the darkening altitude of Twyn Barlwm mountain and the roof-topped hills of Newport, the Severn sea, and the low hills of Somerset beyond. Turning still, the eye travelled along the chimney-woven carpet of the

Cardiff plain, the islands, the shipping, the long widening silvered sea route to the west—and the wind was in my face again.

Unceasingly he roared up the slope and through the beeches, triumphant in his unimpeded might, concentrated on the tiny human dreamer and his dog on the skyline.

Bracken fronds, air-borne, came up on a one-way passage to the peace and calm beyond. Sheep nestled in the shelter of hedge banks and I left them undisturbed. No lark, curlew, peewit or rabbit showed, only a solitary raven passed below me rejoicing in his natural element, the mountain wind, which for that hour I shared with him. I hailed him with a shout, and he side-slipped into the gale with a silvered flash of sunlight on the ebony of his wings. He dived, spun over in raven play, and was gone.

Rain still threatened, but all the while my hill stood out as if gilded, unsullied by the surrounding gloom. At last I turned away from my perch in the teeth of nature's slipstream, and made for the shelter of the woodlands and the lane in the peace of the Nofydd valley.

I paused to light a cigarette and watch the clouds pass on across the blue vault of the sky with their shadows beneath them steeplechasing over the fern-clad hills. I saw and heard the ash trees bending and sighing, while the wind went on singing the song of the mountains as it passed through the bracken, never to return.

The glistening watery lane led downward, and so with Toss at my heels once more, I followed deeper into the heart of the willow glen, where every tree was clouded with a nimbus of pale gold catkins a-shimmer in the sunlight. My soul was happy and renewed from that mad March hour of freedom on the hills.

The greatest test : Toss has been called up to within eight inches of a cornered sheep, and still keeps his head

Toss keeps the flock in position while one of the sheep is caught

A piece of wire entangled with the wool has to be clipped off

Over the sticks

Flock inspection

Driving practice for the trials

Penning practice for the trials

CHAPTER IX

Problems at Lambing Time

ALTHOUGH shepherds are usually sparing of words, unaccustomed to analysing or making much of their emotions, there can be few shepherds who remain unmoved by the sight of their first spring lambs being born. Tough men have often told me that the lambing is the finest time of the year, and I for one cannot but agree with them. Normally I am no fonder than most people of rising in the morning, but in March and April I never have the slightest difficulty in waking early and getting out of bed. The excitement of lambing is more than sufficient incentive. On a lovely April dawn, when the grass is wet and the chorus of blackbirds and thrushes is joined by the migrant warblers, I am at my happiest and so is Toss. Most of the human world is asleep, oblivious of the long ecstasies of birdsong soaring up from the valleys, but I am up betimes, going my rounds with Toss at my heels, with my crook and a bucket of water, and a bottle of warm milk in my pocket.

Sheepdog Glory

The greater part of my flock is usually brought down from the hill some days before the first lamb is due. On the steep reservoir batter (or embankment) in view of my kitchen window, the ewes give up in ones and twos their 'secrets' guarded for five long months.

With the big strong tan-faced Glamorgan sheep, birth troubles are rare, particularly if they have wintered well. As mothers, they have no equal, and provided they are kept on their native ground, the Coal Measures or neighbouring limestone, they will remain equally hardy. It has often been noted with what wisdom, courage and devotion they defend their young, and above all their prolific supply of rich milk helps the rearing of splendid lambs, which, when sired by a Welsh ram, are often on their feet and sucking within forty-five seconds of birth.

How Toss loves the sight of a new-born lamb! As for some loyal member of a large family, the birth of the youngest baby is always an occasion of absorbing interest to him. If for some reason a new lamb has to be separated from its mother for a few minutes, Toss is the happiest dog in the world at being allowed to take charge of it; his presence, if it does nothing else, is at least enough to keep the baby quiet while the mother is attended to.

A shepherd becomes adept at recognising from a distance the stance of a ewe which has lambed during the night. Her head hangs low, but as you approach she looks up in defiance and stamps, sniffs the ground, looks up and stamps again. Then a thin wisp of steam rises from the long grass at her feet and two black heads with long ears pop up at the sound of her stamping. Like a pair of four-legged gollywogs the lambs scramble to their feet and make unerringly for the source of milk. Silently you exult over the happy spectacle, and all the while the mother watches with the cold balefulness of a python about to strike; her courage on the morning of her lambing is something to command respect. On the following day she will have rejoined the flock, and be ready to run with her lambs bobbing along on either side of her; but for this morning she is anchored to her ungainly babies, and wants the seclusion which she has earned. Then follows the sound of contented sucking, the wriggling of tiny tails, an extra shove at the udder. The mother starts to chew the cud, but her eyes never leave Toss, who is as happy and interested as I am. I light a cigarette, and we back quietly away.

The rest of the flock graze peacefully, but at the top of the bank beside the wire netting fence a sheep lies awkwardly. She gets up, looks round at the ground, then lies down heavily again. Her ears twitch backwards, she raises her head high, then rests it on the ground. For ten minutes I watch and wait as she gets up, turns round, walks a few yards, and stops to graze; the movements of her ears betray clearly that she has other things on her mind. She soon lies down again and points her head to the sky. There is no purpose in waiting, she is better left alone.

Before returning to breakfast I take a bucket of water to the freshly-lambed ewe, to be reminded once more of the incredible memory which sheep have. So great is a ewe's thirst after lambing that she will empty half a bucket of water without stopping. Apart from spells of hot dry weather this is probably the only time of the year when she does drink, and certainly the only time when I carry a bucket of water. She might only have seen the bucket once, and that twelve months before, but she recognises it when I am fifty yards away and comes to meet me.

Lunch time finds me on the batter again. The sheep with the twins has moved to another spot, and all three are asleep in the spring sunshine. Single lambs, incidentally, are always bigger than twins, and it is easy to tell after the birth of one lamb whether a second is to be expected.

The ewe by the wire netting fence stands with head down. Her flanks have gone in, and she is preoccupied with something on the ground. She has just lambed, and I rush up to help a big single lamb to struggle out of the steaming and slimy membrane in which it is wrapped. It struggles to its feet, coughing and feebly shaking its drooping ears. I step back and the mother takes over, licking and mumbling the ovine equivalent of 'sweet nothings' to the tremulous quivering little object balanced on its four black stilts of legs. It is too soon for the bucket of water yet, for she will be too absorbed by cleaning and drying her handsome off-spring to bother for a while about her own needs.

The normal run of the season follows this pattern, though all too often the arrival of bitter weather puts a stop to the pleasures of supervision. Deaths occur through various causes, sometimes during the birth of a second lamb; the ever-watching carrion crows and wily magpies often beat the shepherd in the dim light of the early mornings when it is touch and go with a weak lamb. Usually the mother can deal with these predatory birds, and if all is well the babies themselves will totter after the crows when only half a day old; but the nightly raids of a determined fox can play havoc with their numbers.

Lyrical enjoyment is a part of lambing, but the times are not always appropriate for it, and when a new-born lamb is lying cold and trembling, swift measures must be taken to save him. I may need to bring him home to bask in the warmth of the electric fire in the kitchen, with a suck or two from the bottle; and some-times even a spot of brandy and glucose will go down a clammy little throat. Then the lamb is propped up on its legs and supported until it is strong enough to stand by itself, when it can be returned to its mother and both are left together in a shed for half a day.

Sometimes a lamb seems warm enough but for some reason has failed to find the udder; then, if the weather is cold and wet, and the mother young and awkward, the lamb soon dies unless a good long suck can be arranged for it. At such times as this, when the distracted ewe has to be penned for catching, there is immense value in having a strong-eyed dog present. To pen the fretful mother of a stupid unco-operative lamb is a test which only the best dogs will pass.

Toss quickly became an artist at this work. He would steadily advance upon the ewe step by step, and she would have to back reluctantly before the commanding glare of his eyes. I would always be at hand ready to intervene in case the desperate mother should suddenly charge him, either reducing his growing confidence, or else arousing in him an uncontrollable urge to retaliate.

Both lack of confidence and sudden temper are as much to be deplored in a sheepdog as in a schoolmaster, who should be unafraid of his class, maintaining good discipline without having to resort to punishment. It may sound fanciful, but my inside knowledge of the profession and of the breed suggests to me distinct similarities of temperament—may colleagues regard this as the sincere compliment intended—between a first-class schoolmaster and a first-class Border Collie.

I have had dogs who were too scared for this lambing work and others who could not be trusted to remain calm and keep their temper when faced by a butting ewe. Toss at such times has the eyes of a hypnotist and the patience of Job, and so the ewe and lamb are eventually cornered in the shed.

A Night's Shelter for the Newly-born

The weak lamb has then to be held to the udder with one hand, and the tiny mouth engaged on the teat with the other hand. The ewe is held against the wall with knee and thigh, which is an awkward job,

(79)

and it takes time to stimulate the sucking action of the lamb. The shepherd's back and his patience are often tested to breaking point, but at last the little creature gets the hang of it and the milk flow begins to pass from mother to offspring. The sheep's taut body begins to slacken as the colostrom seeps into the lamb. As the warm transfusion goes on, the lamb gradually stiffens, and the little head begins to work between your fingers. The familiar contented sucking sound is heard, a white spot of milky froth shows by the lamb's mouth, and you begin to feel the swallowing action. The ewe is turned and the same process is repeated on the other teat. The lamb's tail begins to wriggle, and soon it is transformed into a vigorous sucking machine. Then the two can be safely left close to each other in the shelter of the shed, and you can steal away contented in the knowledge that another head has been added to the flock.

On returning to release the ewe for grazing, you are greeted by the heart-warming sight of the bright little head looking up from the straw at its mother's side. The tiny creature, which might so easily have died, stands up, arches its back and stretches, giving you a fine reward in the enjoyment of its beauty.

I have often found a strong lamb beside its mother on some bleak exposed place taking the blast of March's early morning winds, and picked it up to carry it to some more sheltered spot. The warmth from its body makes it an agreeable thing to hold for hands which are stiff and chilled. Indeed it makes me feel almost ashamed to be swathed in coats when I feel the warmth of these babies of the open hills and marvel at their hardiness and resilience.

Dry cold seems to worry them very little but a long night's rain spoils the pleasure of the following morning's walk, swiftly toning down any idyllic picture of lambing which the shepherd may normally cherish.

On one particularly vicious evening of sleet and wind, I noticed a young ewe standing alone, a fact which always calls for investigation. On approaching I could see that she had lambed that day, but no baby was in sight. She refused to leave the spot, and it looked as though a fox had robbed us both. She stood

(81)
F

disconsolately beside a rabbit hole, and before leaving I happened to notice a tiny fox-like face framed in the entrance of the hole. So bitter was the wind and sleet that the little lamb had found the sense to crawl or back into the hole for protection from the elements. I have never been more impressed by the instinct for self-preservation in an infant creature still wet from its mother's womb.

Sometimes a ewe lamb is not sold but retained for breeding purposes in which case she and her mother will stay close to each other throughout the year. When they both become mothers in the following spring, they may often still be seen together, each with her own lamb—either because the original mother has a great desire for her grown daughter's company, or the daughter wishes to share with her mother the joy of her own first-born!

On rare occasions a ewe will have nothing to do with her lamb, and there are few more pathetic sights than a lamb feebly trying to keep up with its mother: in a short time, unable to go any further, it will fall a prey to the ever-watchful crows. For some obscure reason the ewe cannot stand having the lamb near her. Perhaps there is some defect in her senses of smell and hearing, the two senses especially concerned with animal recognition. If the sound of the bleat and the scent of the wool fails to stimulate her maternal instinct, this must be awakened for her in another way.

Problems at Lambing Time

She goes into the pen once more. On such occasions
—and only on such occasions—Toss is allowed in as
well. This is an ancient trick of the shepherd's craft,
for the ewe will immediately regard the dog's presence
as a threat of danger to the lamb, and her reaction to
protect it is gradually stimulated. At first it may seem
hopeless, the lamb might not be there for all the notice
she takes of it. Time after time it makes for the udder
only to be brushed aside, and it has to be bottle-fed in
order to survive. At last, however, the threatening
presence of the dog will induce the ewe to accept her
lamb which may have been stumbling round her legs
for hours. Then, provided that there is no painful
udder trouble, another victory has been won.

Difficult and touchy as some of these rescues are,
there are some still more difficult and even gruesome,
as when the ewe's womb itself must be invaded for the
lamb's release.

This happened with one of the grey-faced Radnor
sheep on Cefn Carnau hill. She had not been brought
to the reservoir, and by a lucky chance I came upon
her as she lay alone in the corner of a field. One be-
draggled lamb was bleating miserably by her side and
she was incapable of bringing forth her second:
examination showed that she had lost the strength
needed to bring about its expulsion. Part of its head
was visible, but the two front feet, which should be
aligned with the lamb's nose, were not showing.

Sheepdog Glory

Having only started breeding sheep a few years before, I had so far been spared the need for such a major operation. I had not even seen it done, but luckily had read it all up and knew it at least in theory. It was too early in the morning to go for the vet, or even a neighbour; and anyway it would have taken too long. There were only two courses open to me, to kill the ewe or draw the lamb away—and the first of these alternatives was impracticable, for I had no means of shooting her. The second remained, and there was no time to be squeamish. The born lamb's cries were worrying the poor sheep even in her great agony, so I took it away and gave it a good suck to quieten it, then tied Toss up and presented him with the lamb to lick. He was delighted with this duty, and there was peace for a while.

I returned to where the ewe lay, took off my coat and rolled up my sleeves. Fortunately I had all the necessities in my haversack. As I am a violinist, the fingers on my left hand are stronger and far more supple than those on the right, so I disinfected my left hand and arm.

I then bent down and gently pushed the swollen, shapeless and slippery head back into the womb. Inside, the lamb felt unlike any normal four-legged animal, and I realised afterwards that I had been feeling the extreme suppleness of the unborn.

After intensive contortions with both hands it was

possible to get the head out but without the two front feet; and the shoulders then prevented any further withdrawal. The head had to be pushed in again, and the two front feet drawn out. The disinfected lambing cords were tied to these, and then they were allowed to slip back with the cords left protruding. Then the head was drawn out for the last time.

The poor ewe (fortunately she was a big one) had ceased to strain, the natural birth pains had gone, and she was past giving me any further help. With the ending of the pains the pelvic bones would begin to close, and I thought she would have to be shot in the end. Time was running out.

I gently drew the cords with the feet attached, until nose and feet were within my grasp, and the oily, slippery, slimy thing came away with a sickening gush and flopped on to the grass between my knees.

The lamb was still alive and it might have been possible to save it, but I soon dismissed the urge to try and saddle the mother with twins after what she had been through. If she could rear the strong one, it would be enough for that season.

For over half an hour I had been on and off my knees in the wet grass, the sweat collecting along my eyebrows with the sustained tension of the job. The right hand working on the outside of the abdomen, had been as busy as the left, squeezing and levering the elusive wobbling head into position for a grip with the fingers of the left hand. I straightened my back and looked down at the ewe, as she lay in the aftermath of her agony, and I thought of the people who grumble at the price of lamb, compared with the price she had had to pay. She struggled to her feet, the first lamb tottered up to her, and began sucking vigorously. As she turned to lick him, I found myself practically sobbing with a blend of relief and joy and sadness. A small tragedy had been redeemed by a great personal triumph, which not every farmer can achieve, and somehow I detected a hint of applause in the beat of Toss's tail. Somehow too I could guess at a look of wonder and happiness in his eyes.

I fetched some water, and the old sheep drank and drank. Then, rather stiffly, she walked away with her little one beside her, and before my astonished eyes, she started to graze.

◆◆◆◆◆◆◆◆◆◆◆◆◆◆◆◆◆◆◆◆◆◆◆◆◆◆◆◆◆◆◆◆◆◆◆◆

CHAPTER X

APRIL–MAY

◆◆◆◆◆◆◆◆◆◆◆◆◆◆◆◆◆◆◆◆◆◆◆◆◆◆◆◆◆◆◆◆◆◆◆◆

The Killer's Last Raid

THE SPRING was really the effective beginning of the working partnership between Toss and myself—for his earlier usefulness had been largely incidental; and if our first weeks together had been like a courtship, these weeks in April were something of a honeymoon. I gave him no orders, taught no commands, and set him no problems. The ewes, being heavy in lamb and by now accustomed to dogs, grazed on—giving Toss the perfect introduction to sheep. They accepted at once his wide sweeping runs, and remained indifferent as long as he kept his distance. If this proviso was satisfied, I too was content to remain a passive but watchful spectator.

I had always been on the look-out for any bad habits to show themselves in Toss, but so far none had appeared. A very bad fault in a sheepdog, for instance, is an over-readiness to grip sheep under provocation. Even if the sheep is only gripped by the wool and is not at all hurt, it is an ugly spectacle for gentle 'lay'

audiences, and most judges at trials automatically dis-
qualify the dog in question, which is supposed to
control the sheep in such a way that no situation arises
where he is obliged to grip the sheep. In other words,
if sheep are badly worked and get frightened, one
panicky animal may rush past the dog, who is reduced
as a last resort to stopping it with his teeth. What else
could he do?—But the point is, he should not have
got the sheep into that state in the first place.

As I have said, however, Toss showed no signs of
such 'vice', and in general I felt a good deal of satisfaction over the pattern of his development in these
first months. I had continually kept him out on his
turns; though about five minutes during the morning
and evening was a long enough period at first. As he
gained strength, I extended his running time to the
time it took me to smoke a cigarette. Then I introduced
the stop whistle, the essential foundation on which the
whole complicated science depends.

In training a sheepdog, one must bear in mind the
inbred 'obsession' of the true Border Collie pup: he
must not allow sheep to escape his master. To counter-
act that obsession, he must always be on the far side
of the flock from where the shepherd stands. This is
the instinctive position of power. From this point he
can balance sheep on the imaginary line between himself and his master. Positionally, one is at six o'clock,
and the dog at twelve o'clock.

The Killer's Last Raid

However much the man moves, the young dog automatically adjusts his own position accordingly. If the man moves, the dog moves; if the man stops the dog stops; and if the man gives his stop whistle as he comes to a standstill, the young dog soon learns to associate the whistle with his own cessation of movement.

When this all-important first command has been well learnt, the flanking orders to left or right are given in the same way: sometimes by word of mouth and sometimes by whistles, according to the shepherd's fancy; in whichever form he gives the orders, he must keep them constant in pitch, and insist upon implicit obedience at all times. In the early stages of a dog's training, however, these commands should be given with great care, and only when there is every chance that they will be obeyed.

A popular belief exists that the young sheepdog learns from an old dog by copying his movements. This is an appealing theory, but quite untrue, as the older dog will always want the position of power to himself, and the younger one (provided always that he is ready to work) will align himself at some other point. The man and two dogs then automatically form the points of a triangle. The old dog always claims the bigger share of the work, and the younger one ends up by fussing about in some position where he is neither happy nor wanted. It is at such times that he develops

bad tricks, which once learnt can only be eradicated
with much difficulty.

Of course shepherds are often seen with two dogs of
varying ages, both working together; but this is because both are so keen that it is easier to allow them
this freedom than to struggle with one on a lead. If a
young dog is being coached for high-class competition
work, he must have the field to himself, and the
trainer's undivided attention.

There are considerable variations in the training
methods employed by successful handlers. Some use
ducks, because the instinct of these birds to flock
makes them bunch together like sheep. Some work
with a stuffed sheep, and some have their youngsters
on a long cord. Perhaps all methods work equally well
provided the animal is sensible and willing, and the
shepherd has endless patience. It has always been my
opinion, however, that the young should develop
naturally, even if it takes longer. The final result will
probably be better if nature is given her full time than
if freedom of development is cramped by too many
early restrictions.

I did not hope to train Toss in two months, nor even
in two years, to the pitch of competing satisfactorily
with the finest flower of British sheepdogs. It was more
likely to be four years before the announcement over
the microphone that 'Mr Roy Saunders with Toss is
on the mark' would make the visiting Scottish and

The Killer's Last Raid

English competitors stub out their fag-ends and stop their everlasting talk about dogs, to watch in silence.

My pupil needed no harsh words in those early days, and at that stage his behaviour seemed too good to be true: all the wisdom of the hills and his ancient calling was in him. The evening's training which ended the day's work was a joy to watch, and through the first months of our career together, I could see the harmonious blend of all the required qualities: strength, speed and power, quickness to learn, accuracy, and unswerving affection for his master. My own ewes grew to know his moves so well that at times I almost fancied some of them learnt my commands: as Toss would take a whistle to move to the right, the sheep would veer left accordingly. This became too easy, and in consequence I took a keen pleasure in taking him to neighbouring flocks for ten minutes with sheep which were strange to him. They would respond more quickly, exciting him to a livelier and more stylish performance.

Right from the start, his outrun to gather sheep was the fulfilment of a trialist's dream. It never varied, and he never faltered. Either to the left or right, he could be relied upon to go wide and very fast, coming round well behind the sheep at a slower speed and stopping at twelve o'clock without a command.

To one whose previous experience at trials had been in running headstrong dogs which were difficult and sometimes impossible to stop, this was something beyond price. It developed into a regular form of behaviour pattern as constant as the kestrel's hover or the buzzard's circling glide; and on one unforgettable occasion I used this sure casting run to great personal benefit.

It was during this first lambing season, when all ewes due to lamb in the next fortnight had been brought down from the hill, and enclosed on the reservoir batter near my house. This amounted to some three acres which I had rented from the City Corporation, and fenced off with wire netting from the main storage basin. This was the home 'bucht' (a Scottish term for the part of the farmstead near or around the home buildings), and was quite useful at such times.

One evening the first arrivals showed up, a pair of sturdy black-faced twins. The weather was mild, and there was no occasion to put them into the shed for the first night, as was the practice during rough weather. On the following morning, one of the twins had vanished. The nature of the place was such that had the lamb died I should easily have found it somewhere in the enclosure.

That day several single lambs were born, and there was another pair of twins in the afternoon. Next morning the singles were still with their mothers, but one of the second pair of twins was missing. The mother, a red coarse-haired Glamorgan mountain ewe, one of the toughest things that breathe, was lying down. She rose heavily at our approach, like one who has not slept all night. She glared and stamped at Toss, and at this I noticed the hoof marks on the turf around her: throughout the night she had evidently been stamping and butting in fury. I backed away, and she sank down again exhausted beside her sleepy lamb.

That was my first clue. It was either a fox or a dog, which she had kept at bay for hours. In my part of the world there are far too many killer dogs about, the chief cause, in my opinion, being boredom—for they are invariably mongrels from the mining towns where they are at large during the night. This trouble is at its worst when ewes are heavy in lamb, though it is a mystery how the dogs realise the vulnerability of sheep at that time.

In any case, however, neither dog nor fox, carrying a Suffolk lamb in its jaws, could have jumped the five-foot galvanised mesh fence which formed the boundary. I searched every inch of the boundary fence for a hole through which the killer could have entered, but found none. It was on my second circuit of the fence that I noticed some spots of blood on the grass beneath the netting wire. From the cunning of the entry I felt fairly sure it had been a fox, possibly a vixen feeding her young.

I could see that the same thing would happen each

night, and the fox, assured of an easy and succulent meal, would come again and again. My lamb crop would suffer terribly, not to mention the udders of the bereft ewes, and it was obvious that I had to match my wits against the crafty raider, and put an end to his ravages for ever. The age-old shepherd's instinct for protecting his flock began to take possession of me with increasing power.

Fortunately it was Saturday and I could devote the whole day to planning the fox's death, in which the puppy's outrun was to play its part. At dusk I drew the flock away and put them on the lawn behind the house. One big Radnor ewe with the heart of a lion, who had lambed that day, was left behind as a decoy. Several sacks of straw made a comfortable couch in my shed to which I brought a hurricane lamp, books, and a thermos of tea. I armed myself with a gun and some cartridges charged with No. 2 shot, and Toss was also there, of course, tethered by a stout cord.

I tied the Radnor by a halter, to a stake driven into the ground some twenty yards from the weak point in the wire, and within range from my planned firing

(94)

point. Half-way between the sheep and the fence a
boiled herring invited the killer's entry at that spot.
The stage was set, and my vigil began. Fortunately the
night was mild at first, and I could read, doze and
listen quite happily. There was plenty to listen to: the
squeaking mice, the movement of worms, the sighing
of cattle, the mating call of little owls, the fitful breathing of the sleeping dog, and the distant shunt of trains;
but all the time my ears waited for one sound more
important than all the others, the vicious alarm-snort
of the decoy Radnor.

As the night dragged on, I found myself remember-
ing other nights, in boyhood beside the Towy awaiting
the arrival of migrant geese and duck, flashlight badger
photography, war-time guard-duty with the R.A.F.

As often on those guard duties, nothing happened all night.

About six a.m, however, little Toss suddenly awoke, stood up quickly and looked at the door with no wag in his tail. I slipped two cartridges into the gun, cocked the hammers, and went outside to listen.

The wind was keen as a knife and brought the tears from my sleepy eyes. But from the top of the batter came the sound I had waited so long to hear. The sleeping dog had woken to warn me that the fox was approaching, and the ewe's snort told me that the enemy had arrived.

With thumping heart I scaled the steep slope of the batter, and listened anxiously. I was afraid to peep over, in case the fox should see me and escape. In any case there was no need to risk it, for now the mad stamping and snorting of the ewe left no doubt about the situation.

I unleashed Toss and he sped away to the right along the slope. Dozens of times on the previous afternoon this move had been practised. It was planned so that his run would bring him along the inside of the netting wire, and cut off the fox's escape.

As soon as Toss went over into view of the enemy, he would have about the same distance as the fox had to run to the weak point. As he went over, I peeped. The killer was there all right, and streaking for his exit, but so was Toss, who had a start. The fox saw

his danger, checked, and turned back in my direction.
I let him come—with one finger on each trigger, I let
him come, raising the muzzle to receive him. He was
barely ten yards away when with infinite satisfaction
I squeezed both triggers. A hundred pounds' worth
of lambs might depend on my shot.

Before the last echo of the double explosion boomed
back from the wooded hills, in the dim light of that
Sabbath morning, the fox's quivering had stopped. As
I looked down at the wicked face, distorted by the
nearness of the shot into a mere caricature of a fox,
I ejected the cartridges, and the cordite smoke wisps
drifted away on the morning breeze. It was once again
a place where 'sheep may safely graze'.

◆◆◆

CHAPTER XI

MAY

◆◆◆

Fresh Experiences for a Working Dog

THE lambing ewes ate up the reservoir grass all too quickly, and as soon as the babies were big enough to walk the distance, I had to take them up to my hill. Most of the way was by a narrow winding road where cars were frequent, so I always viewed this journey with some apprehension. It had to be undertaken, however, and each Saturday morning found me shedding off the ewes with strong young lambs and setting off for Cefn Carnau with Toss in command.

I recall now one particular morning. To avoid the traffic, I had made a very early start, calling Toss from his shed as the pre-dawn chorus broke. The fields were white with dew, and when I looked back I could see a double pathway left in the grass by our footprints.

Toss made his usual circuit of the reservoir, the ewes with the bigger lambs were soon separated from the rest, and we set off on the long trek to the rearing ground. As we went down the hill, the sun came up on the curtained bedroom windows of sleeping neighbours. As so often, I felt a little sorry for them: fancy missing this splendid dawn, still fresh with scents of the fading night.

The bird chorus grew to its throbbing climax, and the little band of mothers with their noisy babies moved down into the village; then up the hill road which overlooked Cardiff, still asleep beneath the rising sun. The ewes had spread out, each small woolly baby had found its dam, and they plodded on in groups, tails knocking from side to side, silent at last.

My mood of carefree happiness lasted till I reached the farm where foot-and-mouth had broken out the previous winter. Here I had planned to cross a twenty-acre field to reach the next valley and save the lambs the long trek round by the road. But Emrys had now restocked the farm, and about a hundred sheep were grazing the big field. It seemed foolhardy to try and escort my little bunch of sheep through the field; with only a young dog to keep them apart, the two flocks would run together and intermingle.

I lit a cigarette, and leaned on the gate to think it over. I looked down at the little animal whose prowess I vaunted so much, and he, returning my gaze, seemed to say: 'Can't you trust me this time?' Once I had read that message in his eager face, there could be no refusing the challenge; and the lambs too seemed to add their plea in favour of the short cut. So I decided to risk it, and opened the gate: 'Come on up, Toss boy.

Steady there now.' It was very exciting, for here was a
sporting contest, a super-sheepdog trial—the real thing!
We filed steadily into the arena, but the only spectators were the sheep which barred our way. Toss and I
deployed quickly for the campaign to keep the flocks
apart and get across without mixing. What type of
action should it be: the Charge of the Light Brigade,
or a steady British Square? It resolved itself into a bit
of both.

I formed the spearhead, with Toss weaving a flanking rearguard action to keep his own sheep intact and
close to me. At sight of this show of disciplined resolu-
tion the hosts before us broke and fled, but unluckily
they divided into two halves, which reduced our
chances of success. The little procession went steadily
forward, watched by the hostile gaze of the enemy,
which had stopped and turned to stare. Suddenly, as I
had anticipated, they started to advance. Curiosity had
got the better of them, and now, after our success had
appeared certain, they began to close in steadily upon
us.

I increased speed, which was automatically taken
up by Toss and his charges, but also by the two in-
quisitive flocks on either side. They closed in upon us,
but the flashing movements of the little collie, wheel-
ing and flanking about the animals he knew to be his
responsibility, were enough to keep the strangers back
until we reached the other side of the field. I rushed on,

opened the gate; the ewes and lambs streamed through with Toss at their heels, and I closed the gate full in the faces of the eager followers.

The cavalcade went on and I followed into the valley at a leisurely pace. Toss had scored another hit in my esteem, for right across the field his eyes had never left the sheep he knew so well. His movements to keep them intact had also been enough to keep the strangers at bay, and all my doubts and fears had been unfounded.

The weeks passed, and one little episode after another made my belief in him ever firmer. Certain flaws in his behaviour remained to be cleared up, but I felt that time alone would do this. A more experienced trainer might have put him right on all points in preparation for the approaching season, but I was—or had to be—content to wait on the full and natural development of his confidence. In one way time was on my side—but it might be frustrating to have to wait so long. Yet just as no formula has so far been devised for inducing the early maturity of wine, so fullest development of the Border Collie sheepdog is not reached until the third, fourth, or sometimes fifth year of his short life.

I felt confident at least that my youngster was ready to compete in the best company, without making a fool of his master. We had come a long way together already, and he was a vastly different animal from the dirty little skeleton whose insatiable desire for work had so challenged me at our first meeting.

There was one thing, however, which was essential to his development at this stage: he must have as much experience as possible on strange sheep which moved freely before him. My ewes had grown to know him so well that they were no longer afraid of him, and the way to handle timid sheep is an important factor in the final training of a competition sheepdog. In the approaching trials he would be working on fresh sheep, and keeping the proper distance from them was imperative. To move my own sheep, he had to come in close, but if this were done with some of the wily customers to be controlled in hill trials, things would go badly with us. Few things can make a man feel a bigger fool before a thousand spectators, than to have three or five wild sheep bolting before an eager dog.

Toss's reputation as a long-distance gathering dog spread among the sheep-farmers of the district. I was frequently asked to lend a hand at gatherings on the high Glamorgan hills or along the foreshore. These men knew that I valued the experience which Toss received under fresh conditions of work on new terrain. But most of all I revelled in the way he beat the hill dogs at their own game, and on their own territory. Over Caerphilly mountain, Craig yr Allt, and the Garth mountain itself—distance was no object if sheep had to be gathered.

Fresh Experiences for a Working Dog

In the tenancy of the Deri Farm at Rhiwbina were the grazing rights of a tract of foreshore between the Cardiff-Newport sea-wall and the channel. Some of the Tredegar estate farms, of which the Deri was one, included the grazing of this nutritious 'tack' land as an ancient privilege. My good neighbour, Mr George of the Deri, grazed his marsh with a flock of black-nosed Kerry Hill sheep, and on many a spring evening I drove him and his shepherd down to inspect the flock.

It was a wide expanse of turf over which the stock fed, and as Toss went to work, the sheep-flecked moor sprang to life. Ewes and lambs on the outer fringes would spurt away before his curving outrun and make for the centre, as he ran on—looking smaller and smaller along the distant perimeter. The sheep flocked inwards toward the centre of the circle which his path described. When completely bunched, the woolly mass would come bobbing freely towards us, to be gathered into the wire fold for the shepherd's attention.

My job over, I would sit on the sea wall and listen to the wild calling of the sea birds: the piping of oyster-catchers, the cackle of sheldrake, the fluting of curlews, the wail of plovers, the sharp cry of redshank and yodelling of gulls. A confused babble of music from the distant tide-line never failed to induce in me a drowsy tranquillity of mind.

On one occasion the restless movement of migrating birds came in from the sea, heading inland for dispersal to their nesting grounds. Neither the flockmaster nor his shepherd saw them pass, and certainly the panting and filthy Toss, crouching in the grey mud, never let his gaze wander from the penned sheep. The aerial cavalcade swept on in tired silence, with only an occasional twitter from some warbler or pipit as it passed on its blind instinctive urge to fulfil its destiny on British soil.

So rarely does one get the chance of witnessing a part of this great mystery, the world movement of birds, that I gladly forgot the shepherds in the coming of so many winged visitors from Africa. It was not spectacular in the usual sense, only quiet desultory groups of tiny birds coming in from the channel and following the course of the Rhymney river. Thousands of others would be doing the same thing at river mouths all along the flyways of the northern hemisphere, ensuring easy and natural distribution.

Much information has already been gathered on migration routes, but the real mystery of it still remains. The nomads of the sky still go unfettered and unchecked across the man-made frontiers of the world, their wings a passport to anywhere. In a million years they will still be travelling by the same flyways, and we who watch the age-old miracle, the shy movement of the warblers, the noisy gathering of the swallows, formation skeins of wild geese passing over in the night, must pause and wonder at their 'briefing'.

My two friends and Toss applied themselves to their task with a single-mindedness which for the time being shut me out. Their work was of great urgency, for some of the ewes showed the attack of blow-fly. The

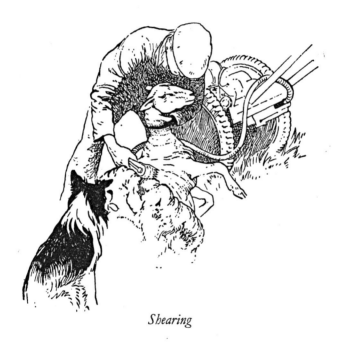

Shearing

practised eye could recognise the presence of maggots in the disturbed patches of wool which had to be clipped away so that a dressing could be applied to prevent further 'strike'.

A stage in the life-cycle of birds passed overhead, and a stage in the life-cycle of the blow-fly was going on under the fleeces of the two sheep. Fortunately they had been caught in time, and the sheep would be none the worse, but had we come two days later, the maggots would have sucked the oil from the wool, quickly reaching the skin and gradually eating into the flesh. Large numbers of flies, attracted by the smell, would follow the flock, and immeasurable agony would be visited upon the defenceless creatures, before death would release them from their torment.

Such is the value of a clever sheepdog in gathering flocks throughout the spring. Not until the oily fleeces are clipped away, and the ewes are shorn and clean, can the shepherd afford to miss his daily visit. His first ally in the fight must always be the sheepdog, for not until the stricken sheep is penned and caught can the suffering and the danger be arrested.

CHAPTER XII

The Trials Season at Last

AT LONG last the summer trials season opened, the eagerly awaited day of the first competition was at hand. The shepherds would be out with their veteran dogs, their middle-agers and—of particular interest every June—their youngsters. As usual, much money had been invested on promising youngsters during the winter, and now their testing first season was upon them.

On Whit-Monday morning I found little time or inclination for breakfast, and with Toss on the back seat of the car I sped over Caerphilly mountain and along the western valleys of industrial Monmouthshire. Beyond Brynmawr I crossed the mountain barrier which marks the northern limit of the coalfield, then descended to the broad acres of the Vale of Usk and Breconshire, some of the finest landscape scenery in Britain. I was making for the village of Cwm du in a lovely pass at the edge of the Black Mountains, where the year's first sheepdog trial is usually staged.

Sheepdog Glory

Whatever inner confidence I had built up during the training of Toss over the autumn, winter and spring, it disappeared rapidly as I took in my first view of the immense trial field at Cwm du, and thought of the wily sheep and the ticklish job of guiding them between hurdles—for at this trial the competitor is condemned to work in the South Wales Style.

The tests in the South Wales Style have absolutely no bearing on practical sheep husbandry. In this Style a Maltese cross is formed from eight hurdles two feet apart, and the three sheep have to be steered through first one way and then the other at right angles. After this they must be driven through another pair of hurdles standing parallel and also about two feet apart —and what shepherd in his senses would try to coax sheep to do this on his home territory? Then the run is completed by penning them in a tiny triangular pen composed of three hurdles. The style is unpopular with competitors and public alike, and it upsets dogs being trained for the National Style, where the tests are designed to examine the real qualities of the dog. When the sheep refuse to go between the hurdles, there is a sort of stalemate, and the public loses interest. The South Wales Association of Sheepdog Trials is slowly but surely influencing the organisers of trials to adopt the National Style instead, and as one village committee after another joins the Association, each season brings its fresh crop of converts.

The Trials Season at Last

It was early when I reached Cwm du, the sun was hot, but the grass was still wet with dew in the shelter of the hedge where prospects were being discussed.

'How are the sheep running?'

'Damned awful, can't settle them.'

Some of the 'top-notchers' had already failed, so it was anybody's day.

At the far end of the field a flock of sheep, fresh from the mountain, were enclosed in a big pen, and screened from view. When the starter waved his flag, the two men at the pen would catch three sheep and release them in view of the distant competitor who waited with his dog 'on the mark'.

I went out to the mark with distinct forebodings, but Toss, beside me, was eager to be off. The time-keeper set his stop-watch: the whole thing had to be completed in eight minutes. Toss went away in his usual wide sweep to the far end of the field to 'hook' the sheep and 'lift' them. He refused to stop at my first whistle. I gave him a second, which brought him to a standstill, but his refusal at the first command had ruined everything. The sheep had been startled, and they came down the field at nearly the same speed as he had gone round it. The whole course of the run depends on a gentle start, so this was a disastrous beginning.

I rushed to meet the three wild denizens of the Black Mountains as they bore down upon me, and managed to stop them by the Maltese cross. I called Toss round, but the sheep were already scared, and we had lost our chance of completing the run in the smooth gentle way which is required. They would not settle, and you could tell from their faces that they were in a panic every time Toss moved.

There was no point in continuing. This first run was too important an affair for a young dog, and I was afraid he would develop wrong moves in his excitement. Before the time-keeper announced that my time was up, we piloted the sheep away and I penned them with the other used sheep behind the spectators.

Once again I had relearnt the fundamental lesson that the first stop command must be obeyed. Once sheep are frightened, it becomes impossible to carry out the delicate manœuvres necessary to complete the tests. It was no use blaming the sheep, and no use blaming Toss; I must blame myself for having brought him out too young. Yet his work at home had been so good, and why should he have refused now the one all-important command?

Cwm du was not the only trial that day; there was another, held in conjunction with an agricultural show, at a place called Penllergaer, near Swansea.

I needed no advice from the Cwm du people, my course was as clear as crystal. I set off for Swansea with a grim purpose. We had made a bad start, Toss and I, and he had no business to be as far out as his showing that morning had indicated. His quality of work was high; his breeding, his temperament and his careful training had qualified him in my own mind to do much better; but after all it was his first day, and perhaps I was expecting too much.

I soon shook off the dust of Cwm du and headed west for Brecon. It was very hot, and Toss sat on the back seat still panting from his run, with saliva continually dripping on to the seat between his front paws. Having retrieved the sheep, he had done his job as far as he knew, and with most young dogs that was as much as could be hoped for at such an early stage. How could I get across to him the urgency of my needs, my ambitions for his success?

All along the lovely valley of the Usk, bank-holiday parties parked and picnicked beneath the trees. I was hungry too, but there was no time to stop for such trivial things as food. The Brecon road led on past Llandovery to Llandilo, where I stopped for twenty minutes at the farm of an old friend—not so much for a 'social visit', as to use his sheep to make it clear to Toss that he *must* stop at my first whistle. After demonstrating this vital point in no uncertain manner —which Toss seemed to have understood—I set out again, feeling much happier, on the Swansea road, until I came to the popular bank-holiday show-ground at Penllergaer.

Here the sheepdog arena was staged on a small field

adjoining the show. Magnificent Hereford and Friesian cattle, hunters and lovely Welsh ponies—none of these 'showpieces' might have been there for all the notice I took of them.

I pulled up as near to the trials field as possible, and got out to reconnoitre. If Cwm du had been lonely and deserted, this place was alive with people. Round the jumping ring and the sheepdog arena thousands of spectators were watching. Toss had never seen such crowds before, and he was beside himself with joy at the sight of so many children. His love of children is often embarrassing to me, and the younger they are the more he loves them. He seems unable to resist the contents of a pram, he simply must put his paws on the edge and take a quick look inside—before the mother's yell sends him away.

I put him on the lead while I made the necessary entries at the secretary's tent. I was eligible for two runs, as two separate classes were open to me. Unfortunately, as at Cwm du, the South Wales style was being used.

Many old friends were present, and after the customary salaams came the inevitable question: 'What's the young dog like?' I had already bragged too much about him, and the morning's setback in Breconshire had rather knocked the stuffing out of me. So although I still had great confidence in Toss, I was now a good deal more cautious. I shrugged my shoulders, replied that he was a goodish youngster, and left it at that; but this time, when my turn came, it was obvious from the start that the goodish youngster was much more than that.

I walked to the starting place and gave him the long-practised priming words to prepare him for the out-run—'Can you see them?' He had seen them all right, and with the whistled order to start, went wide and fast round the edge of the field to sweep behind the three sheep—and stop at the first command as though he had been shot. The ewes came quietly down the middle of the field and he followed gingerly at the right distance and at the right pace. The little cavalcade came steadily on to pass between the two hurdles set in the middle of the field, and my heart was singing as I watched him come in a half crouch, ears cocked forward and eyes aflame. Here at last was the animal I had been seeking for so long.

The crowd was still and silent. They knew and I knew that here, so far, was the winning run. Perhaps some of them realised they were witnessing the birth of a champion. The sheep, however, looked touchy and ready to 'fly off the handle' the moment that Toss increased his pace.

One of the great qualities needed in a champion is the ability to adjust his speed to that of the particular type of sheep being handled. Slow heavy breeds must be pushed along, wild mountain types must be shadowed gently from a respectful distance. Lucky indeed is the man whose dog automatically sums up the movements of his sheep and adjusts his own movements accordingly. Normally the handler adjusts his dog's movements to those of the stock, but that can only be done with experienced dogs in the 'postgraduate' stage.

The Maltese Cross

At the Maltese cross the three sheep were quietly worked through in both directions. Then one of them upset things by bolting, evidently unable to stand the situation any longer. She stood as much chance of escape as a pigeon from a peregrine falcon, and in a matter of seconds she was collected and swept back·to her waiting friends, amidst a murmur of approval from the tense crowd. But this sheep would now take time to cool down again, and unfortunately I could not give her that time. The stop-watch would be ticking in the hand of the time-keeper, my eight minutes would soon be up, and there were still two obstacles to complete.

Very gingerly Toss escorted them on to the pair of parallel hurdles two feet apart, through which they

The Middle Lane

had to be driven on their way to the triangular pen. At the mouth of the lane formed by these two hurdles one ewe looked nervously at Toss, another looked

(115)

nervously towards the open field, and I looked very nervously at all of them and at the tiny pen beyond. I thought about the ten-pound prize but far more about the thrill of winning this open championship class with my little youngster on his first day out. But the ewes stood baffling and blocking our road to speedy stardom. If I raised my crook or frightened them the

The Last Test: South Wales Style

(116)

slightest bit, they would bolt, and a clean and beautiful run would be spoilt.

If you want a sport which will test nerves, patience and self-control, there is something to be said for one where a ten-pound prize hangs in the balance of whether a sheep will go quietly one way or bolt another. It might be compared to the sight of a ten-pound note floating on the surface of a river: you lean out to reach it as far as you dare, knowing that if you grab too suddenly, you will fall in and drown. The money passes, momentarily brushing your finger tips, is washed on, and lost for ever.

My prize had not yet passed beyond my grasp: the ewes had cooled down, though one of them shuffled and looked round. Toss crouched like a panther in the fresh green aftermath of grass which follows the carting of the hay, and the crowd waited. I gently tapped the ground, and one ewe turned her head to face the lane. I took a pace backward to give her confidence to go. She went quietly, and the other two followed her through. Then on to the pen—would there be enough time? There was another pause, and one at a time they meekly walked in, to the accompaniment of applause which shook the field.

I was not given long to bask in my glory, for Tom Cornelius of Ogmore went to the mark, and brought his three sheep quietly through all the obstacles without a hitch at any point. The touch-line critics relegated me to second place. Then Bill Miles of Treharris was on the mark, with his twelve-year-old veteran dog, Wally, and the critics placed him second to Cornelius—which pushed me to third place. The three runs in that class remained unbeaten, and the final verdict of the judge confirmed our own.

In the other class, Toss kept to the same form, his run was almost identical, and he was placed second.

The homeward journey when a prize has been won always seems half the distance, but when two prizes have been won at the same trial, and that on a puppy's first day out in competition with champions, the miles seem to flash by in a few minutes.

During the rest of June and July, a limited number of Saturday field trials took place, on the broad acres of Breconshire, the Vale of Glamorgan, the Forest of Dean, and the Coal Valley of Ystradgynlais, Newport and Swansea. Toss won a second prize at Bwlch, a third at Ystradgynlais, a first with silver cup at Newport, a third at Swansea, first and second divided at Cardiff, and a second with silver cup at Aberaman. It was a very good start, and he was generally regarded as a serious danger to his rivals. Yet I realised that he was still very 'green' and puppyish, and I knew well enough all the time how far off the ideal were his performances in these early contests.

I have been happy to record his successes, but there were failures as well, both in Toss and in his trainer.

Sometimes he would 'turn sticky' and refuse to obey a flanking command, to move out from the straight line behind the sheep which he loved to keep. But if they were already out of line, a wide flanking move on his part would be essential to swing them back into it, his refusal would cause the sheep to pass outside the two hurdles in the middle of the field, and the name of Toss would be missing from the prize list.

There were many other baffling and exasperating lapses and flaws—such as are almost bound to occur when three determined parties are opposed. The man and the sheep are diametrically opposed to start with, and the dog, the essential 'go-between', is torn between two claims on his obedience: the imposed commands of his handler, and his own reflexes. The sheep form a trio of swift-moving individualists, for however keen they may seem on sticking to each other's company, one of them will always be looking for an opening to escape.

It was, therefore, not surprising that I often felt frustrated on the journey home. The degree of frustration I felt simply because Toss and I had not been on the prize list might seem out of proportion—if it were not for the equally disproportionate happiness to which I was transported a few hours later, in the early sunlight of a summer's dawn on the training fields at home—a happiness which strangely obliterated the disappointments of the previous day.

Out on the mark at midday, with the fight on, before the public, and in the heat of competition, you battle grimly for the prize. You have a goodish run—the best so far, they say in the beer tent. After tea Bill Miles turns up, and with a spanking run puts paid to whatever chances you had of coming first. Dai Daniels does a better run than Miles, and you are down to third. Before the final verdict is announced, John Evans arrives late from some far-distant trial, with a carload of champion dogs, and his first run puts you down to fourth. You know there are only three prizes, but just the same you glance at the catalogue to make certain. There *are* only three.

The long road home calls you away before the verdict is announced, you know it anyway as far as you are concerned. Your pocket has been lightened through petrol, food and entry fees. You set out full of pride and nervous energy, and—now you are returning with only a headache and a general feeling of soreness: returning to the eager questions of a little son.

'Any luck today, Dad?'

'No.'

'Bad sheep, were they?'

'No.'

'Did Toss do anything wrong?'

'No.'

You would have to explain that you lost a drive,

and three points, because you were a fraction of a second late in giving an order; and this is something you do not feel like explaining at all.

Then through a night of dreams you ramble, winning and losing, with booming loudspeaker, whistled commands, clapping spectators, the endless arguments, criticisms and banter inseparable from the eager talk of the partisans of any sport.

With the first note of the blackbird on the apple tree you wake again, and rise to dress and greet the early sun in the freshly scented dawn of a new day. A pot of tea, then Wellingtons and a walking stick, and Toss will be once more running the home stretch, soothing the burnt-out disappointment of the mind with an exhibition far surpassing the finest things which beat you on the day before.

We climb steadily to the Wenallt top, Cardiff's hundred-acre wooded hill park, from where my fields are visible three-quarters of a mile away across the Nofydd valley. We pause at the end of the park to sight the sheep. Toss is ready, I prime him to make certain he has seen them, then he is away. I stand and watch.

Across Councillor Watson's clover he goes in a cloud of dew, where once he trudged behind me in the snow, down the reseeded slope and out of the sunlight, through the farmyard before the bailiff is up, and into the uncut hay beyond, with barking sheepdog and

golden cocker on his heels. Down at the river he shakes
them off, and is lost to view as he climbs the track
through the woods; then round the corn like Mase-
field's fox, and over the gate to the ruined farm, across
my six acres to clear the fence—always onward and
upward. The moving spot reaches the sunlight again,
round the five-acre field to lift the flock beneath the
beeches at the top of the opposite hill: three-quarters
of a mile in one free, eager movement. I wonder with
a smile what Daniels, Evans and Miles would have
thought had they seen it.

Then, like a bunch of tiny maggots fleeing at the
touch of oil, the flock stream into the morning sun on
the steep five-acre field. My game of chess by remote
control has begun.

Guiding the sheep for half an hour to any required
part of the field, moving the tiny dot that is a dog by
voice and whistle from three-quarters of a mile away,
I regain my tranquillity and self-esteem. I am happy
once more, at peace with the world and myself, proud
possessor for that half hour at least of the finest sheepdog in the world.

●◆●◆●◆●◆●◆●◆●◆●◆●◆●◆●◆●◆●◆●◆●◆●◆●◆●◆●◆

CHAPTER XIII

AUGUST

●◆●◆●◆●◆●◆●◆●◆●◆●◆●◆●◆●◆●◆●◆●◆●◆●◆●◆●◆

The Scottish Invasion Week

THE first week of August in South Wales provides a severe test for one who fancies he has the finest sheepdog in the world. For in the six days starting with the Bank Holiday, a festival of trials is held, and the art of sheepdog handling, usually practised in great loneliness, becomes a spectacle for enthusiastic crowds, whose hearts are won by these dogs and their grace and skill in action. Prize money is high, and as some ten different competitions are crammed into this one week, a large entry is attracted, with the best men and dogs from England and Scotland as well as Wales.

There is a formidable group of competitors from England—Messrs Bagshaw, Priestly, Wallace, Denniff and company—but we usually regard this especially as 'Scottish invasion week', and it is a great pleasure to give a strong Welsh welcome, after their long journey down from the Highlands, to these fine sportsmen of the heather, men like Hogarth, Murray, Dixon and Little, Wilson, Anderson and Hislop, Bonella, Mc-

Pherson, McClure, McPhee and Mr Crabb a Scottish schoolmaster.

They come by car, with a crook and a brace of collies apiece, but without any of the usual Caledonian 'accessories', such as the kilts and tam-o-shanters of rugby football supporters. Yet in their speech and personalities they bring a freshness and a bracing atmosphere of their northern heather-clad solitudes, and we are happy to have them with us again. We have learnt much from their visits, and although a Welsh 'partisan' may claim that their wins are becoming fewer, they have certainly in the past carried off a substantial part of the prize money; very little of which, one imagines, ever reaches the Bank of Scotland. Not, in any case, that the visitors are interested only in prize money; for a victory in one of the South Wales August-week trials is a proud achievement for any competitor whatever his country of origin.

The Monday competitions at various centres are usually conducted in the South Wales Style (using three instead of five sheep), and are little favoured by the visitors. They usually arrive on the following day, having competed or given exhibitions with their dogs at various centres on the way, to compete at Cardiff for the first time on the Tuesday, when the National Style of working is introduced.

I shall remember that particular Tuesday, the day after August Bank Holiday, for a very long time.

The Scottish Invasion Week

Organised by Mr Tom Davies, the city's Recreation Officer, the trials were being staged, as is customary for the Tuesday of that week, on Sophia Gardens Field beside the River Taff in the spacious grounds of the city centre—a lung of freshness about the size of London's Hyde Park. It makes a beautiful setting, this field ringed with chestnut paling and splendid elm trees stretching away to Pontcanna, Blackwier and the Castle.

The sheep are brought into the city by lorry and penned at the far end of the field. The hurdles are erected in pairs at two corners of the big triangular course round which the five sheep (released for each competitor) must be driven by his dog.

And so the stage is set, as it was set this year, with Albert Edmunds, one of the Welsh National Trials judges, sitting at his table in the tent, sharpening his pencil ready for the deduction of points. (There are few more soul-destroying sounds for a competitor than the sound of a pocket knife sharpening a pencil in the judge's tent.)

D. H. Rees was at his post testing the loudspeaker and calling for competitors. The time-keeper's watch was carefully wound—for each run must be timed to the second (other stop-watches are used by friends of each competitor, and little mercy is shown towards organisers when a slip is made in timing or judging). I was one of the first competitors in the class for dogs and men who have not yet reached championship class; there was also an open championship class for established handlers in the National Style with championship dogs.

Before going on to my own part in the day's drama, it may be as well to recapitulate the stages in a National Style trial. The handler must remain on his mark and

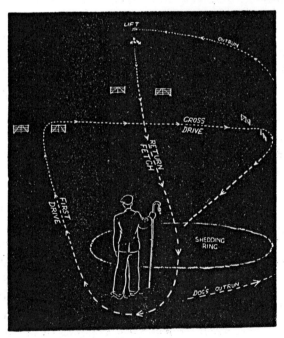

The Course for the National Style

give his commands to flank and guide the dog on its fetch, drive and crossdrive, to enable him to steer his five sheep between each pair of hurdles at the far end of the triangular course. At the final stages of the run he is entitled to move out and assist the dog to complete the last three tests: parting off two sheep, penning the five, and finally singling out the ribboned sheep.

The stage, then, was set, the curtain was about to go up, and there was I in the wings, one of the first actors to 'go on'—a somewhat awe-inspiring position as any participant in amateur dramatics can testify. Course Director Ted Miles escorted me to 'the mark' (a post a few yards in front of the judge's tent) and whispered some words of encouragement in my ear.

Suddenly five white specks appeared against the backcloth of elms at the other end of the park; my sheep were out and Toss was away. Following the wide curve of the palings, he went wide behind his sheep and brought them steadily back between the mid-field hurdles. This was followed by the first drive away, and straight between the hurdles at the end of the drive; then across the field to the right, between the next pair, and back to where I waited at the shedding ring. The two sheep were soon parted from the other three, the five were united again and penned. Toss spun round the pen as I let them out, the marked sheep was quickly singled and turned away, and in that moment I found full reward for all my year's work on him. I could see then that he was heading for the form of a champion, and I also knew that out of the sixty dogs in his class on the field that day, there were few who could put up such a run.

The Critics

Apart from the suspense of waiting for the results, my 'ordeal' was over, and it was extremely pleasant to be able in this mood to enjoy the rest of the day, the bright sunshine, the other performances in my class and the runs in the champions' class, the banter and arguments of the visitors, and at midday—with an hour's relaxation from concentration and rivalry—a splendid lunch in the Banqueting Hall of Cardiff

Castle, to which the Lord Mayor had invited all competitors. We left our dogs and entered by the Black Gate, over Castle Green, and up the steps to the fantastic vaulted Hall and 'the festive board'.

I sat back to watch and listen to that strange assortment of men gathered from the remotest parts of Britain, eating and joking in Cardiff's romantic treasure house, Highland accents mingling with voices from the Border Counties of England and from West, Mid and South Wales. It was indeed an unusual gathering, which perhaps would have seemed almost incredible to previous generations. I reflected how unlike it was to the countries whose workers have attained, only through bloodshed and revolution, to the seats where aristocracy once ruled. Here the shepherds were the Lord Mayor's guests by virtue of their skill and patience with the animals they loved, and because their work gave exciting yet harmless public entertainment.

The laughter and the jokes went on, and eventually we returned to the tourney-field—like the knights of old going out beneath the portcullis in the age of chivalry! Instead of plumed lances and caparisoned chargers, our accoutrements merely amounted to a shepherd's crook and a willing dog. Instead of the fanfare of trumpets heralding the next joust of arms, came the voice of D. H. Rees over the loudspeaker calling for the next competitor!

I

The afternoon passed, and at last the Committee Chairman, Mr John Rees, came into our tent with a piece of paper in his hand—the list of winners to be announced to the waiting journalists. Conversation stopped, and all ears were strained to catch the names being dictated.

First and second prizes were divided between Toss of Cardiff, and Mick, a dog from Cumberland worked by Mr A. McPhee, a veterinary surgeon. Third prize went to a dog trained and worked by John Day, a coalminer from the Swansea valley. That dogs worked by a schoolmaster, a vet and a coalminer, should beat the shepherds at their own game, seemed to have considerable news value, to judge by press reports on the following day, and I felt that Toss had well deserved his first experience of publicity, not to say fame, almost on his own doorstep and barely three miles from the farm where I had first set eyes on him.

The next day found the same competitors on the trials field at Bailey Park, Abergavenny, where three mountains—Blorenge, Skyrrid and Sugar Loaf—look down on the summer scene. The town turned out to watch, tense and absorbed, and though superficially it might have seemed the same old thing taking place all over again, in fact there was no monotony. There never is, for no dog ever gives the same performance two days running.

On the Thursday, the scene shifts to Chepstow's

great agricultural show with its sylvan background of parkland. Everything is different, only the men and the dogs are the same, as they gather in the shade of the oak trees for the men to talk and study the form and craft of their life-long rivals. For once the thrill of controlling a Border Collie has taken root, there is no turning back.

The glory of the sheepdog grips one for life, and sometimes when I am standing in my best green suit in the shade of the trees, on a glorious summer's day at a trial, my mind goes back to the previous winter with its frosts, rain and snowstorms, to the feeding of my flock, to the lambing and its problems—foxes, crows and magpies; to the footrot, shearing, worming, dipping, tailing, branding and earmarking, raddle, bluestone, dip and stockholm tar, to the fear of deadly foot-and-mouth, to the hedging, fencing, slagging, de-thistling, and the continual losing battle with the fern.

In all these toils and perils there is one helper only, my companion, servant and partner, sheepdog Toss. His eagerness, affection and obedience is mine for the snapping of a finger, and his faithfulness is the only thing which never changes in this ever-changing year. When that year's work is almost done, and the lambs are grown and ready for dispatch, the shepherd takes his holiday. It revolves round the sport of his dog without which, that year's work could never have been done. . . .

A burst of applause breaks into my reverie, recalling me to the tournament, and I have to ask a friend how the run has gone.

On the Friday and Saturday of that hectic week there is usually a two-day trial organised by the South Wales Association of Sheepdog Trials, of which I have the honour of being Chairman.

This Association was formed in 1950 and set itself the task of co-ordinating the numerous trials throughout South Wales which were prepared to affiliate. There was an immediate response among societies and private individuals, and the membership grew rapidly. We enlisted the aid of farming journals, the press and the radio: *The Western Mail*, *The Farmer and Stockbreeder*, the *Farmer's Weekly*, and the Welsh Region of the B.B.C. were particularly helpful. The Association gathered momentum, and to stimulate local interest, public meetings were held at Chepstow, Newport, Aberdare, Carmarthen, Abergavenny, Pontypridd, and Builth Wells.

As so often in such organisations, most of the 'donkey work' was carried out by an indefatigable secretary, Mr Gordon Allen of Abergavenny, whose three-page monthly bulletins of Sheepdog News were enjoyed by members in many parts of the British Isles. The present Secretaries, Mr and Mrs Glyn Evans of Aberyscir, near Brecon, are proving extremely worthy successors to Mr Allen, and with their grand work the Association seems likely to go on from strength to strength.

Our trials are staged each year in a different town—so far they have been at Porthcawl, Brecon, Neath and Bridgend. For those of us who go the round of many competitions organised by others, it is an unusual—and stimulating—experience to be taking full command at our own trial: to be flagging out the sheep, timing each competitor, making announcements over the loudspeaker, fussing over the judges, welcoming distinguished visitors, giving drinks to the press, paying homage to the Mayor, and chasing stray dogs off the course!

On these two days the competitors from Caledonia —and England—make their final bids for the Welsh awards. Away go the dogs of international repute, which have run on most of the public trials fields of Britain between Brighton and John o' Groats, dogs like David Murray's short-coated Roman-nosed Vick, Hogarth's sharp-eared Sweep, McClure's wee Meg, David Dickson's Ben; each in his own fashion going round the course on his outrun, to make his final run before setting off on the long road home, back to the heather and the hills for the remainder of the year.

At last the busy week is over, and those of us who have dared to pit our feeble skill against the champions may count the cost. High entry fees from 'the many' have contributed towards the splendid cash prizes and silver cups won by 'the few'. For without the generous sporting instincts of large numbers of competitors who down put their pound note in entry money, the big prizes could not be offered, and there would probably be less stimulus to breed, pick, and train these great little animals.

During the six days of intensive watching, we all learnt many lessons. In my case it had been made very clear that to steer sheep in a straight line between the distant hurdles, the dog must walk. Being a small but extremely lively dog, Toss did not like walking; he preferred a gentle trot. My next job was therefore to try and reduce this trot to a walk, and I had five days in which to do it. On the following Friday I was due to run him at the Welsh National Trials, held that year at Caernarvon.

'Six days shalt thou labour, and do all thy work: but the seventh day is a sabbath . . . in it thou shalt not do any work, thou nor thy son, nor thy daughter, thy manservant, nor thy cattle . . .' The commandment says nothing about sheep and dogs, and at any rate, in the early dawn after the Scottish and English invaders had left us for another year, long before my family or neighbours were astir, Toss and I were once more afield, preparing for summer's greatest day.

◆◆◆

CHAPTER XIV

To the Welsh National Trials

DURING August these National Trials are held in England, Scotland and Wales, and a team of twelve is picked at each of the three Trials. The three teams meet at the International Trials in September, where the thirty-six dogs are run off against each other on a Friday. From them the twelve highest-pointed (irrespective of country) are chosen to compete on the following day in the supreme championship. To secure a place in even the national team must be considered one of the greatest achievements anywhere in the world for co-operation between men and animals, for in no form of animal training is the animal separated from his master by nearly half a mile of open country—with whistled orders to be interpreted and executed at this distance so as to control the movements of five puzzled unco-operative, fast-moving mountain sheep.

At the back of my mind lurked the tantalising hope that some day Toss would be included in the International. It would take years of training, but the chance was surely there. He was certainly a dog of international class, but what about his trainer? Let me admit here and now that I was the weaker half of this partnership; and at any rate I had far more confidence in Toss's ability than in my own.

For several years I had been putting the blame on either the disobedience of my dog or the incredible stupidity of the sheep. When things went wrong it was always the fault of one or the other, never my own. Oh dear no, I was quite above reproach in my own estimation. Eventually it penetrated my thick skull that the behaviour of sheep drawn at a trial in August is fairly well governed by the way a master has trained his dog during the previous eleven months. The reaping depends upon the sowing.

If the dog is continually and relentlessly trained to go out wide, stop at the first command, and retrieve quietly, then the sheep usually respond accordingly. The tests may then be completed with the minimum loss of points. But you are not always told these things as a novice, for there are some hardened trialists who make a point of never giving advice to novices on how to improve themselves and their dogs. That sort of competitor will be more likely to say 'hard luck, Saunders,' with a self-satisfied smirk, and leave it at that. It took the natural accuracy of little Toss to teach me the intricacies of the game, and the necessity for hard and continuous homework.

What is more, I came slowly but surely to the knowledge that in this homework I must keep patient at all costs. It was all too easy to shout at the dog for some fault or refusal to obey, when all the time I knew deep down that this lapse was mainly due to my own inefficient teaching. It was a hard school, but I gradually became inured to the most exacting limits of self-control, combined with unremitting firmness. The dog was doing his best, after all, and sometimes I realised that my tone was too cold and changed over to a coaxing plea in order to give him the essential ounce of encouragement; if he did not do something when he felt threatened, he might do it to please his master. But the sheepdog brain is a mystery, into which not even the wisest master can hope to penetrate completely, however hard he may try.

'Going to run him in the National, Roy?' I was asked that so often in Toss's first summer that I began thinking seriously about the trip to Caernarvon where the trials were being held that year. Of course Toss did not stand an earthly chance of getting into the team, but we both needed the experience, Harold Hawken insisted, and if we made a good impression it would stand to our credit another time. This seemed sound advice and in the end I decided to 'have a go'.

At three a.m on the great day, therefore, I called Toss from his bed of straw, and we set off northwards in the good old Morris Minor along the valley of the Taff, over the Brecon Beacons, down to the Usk, on across the Eppynt Hills to Builth and the mist-choked valley of the Wye.

(137)

Sheepdog Glory

Toss slept soundly on the back seat, oblivious of the maze of rabbits which criss-crossed the road in the beam of my headlamps as we raced on into the darkness, through the gap in the Rhayadr hills and on towards Plynlimmon. Over the Severn valley came the first faint flush of the dawn in the sky, and I thought of the prayer before the battle of Naseby:

> *Oh Lord, Thou knowest how busy we must be this day. If we forget Thee, do not Thou forget us.*

From Llanidloes I steered eastward to Caersws, and then, owing to the freak conformation of the road from South to North Wales, had to turn sharp westward for Machynlleth in the Dovey valley. Northward again into the rocky fastness of the Cader Idris group of mountains, where full daylight brought thousands of sheep to be watched by the two brown eyes from the back seat of the tireless little car.

At the head of gloomy Tal y llyn pass, I stopped to drain the contents of my thermos flask, and drill young Toss for twenty minutes on the slopes of Cader. Then on again through Dolgelly, Trawsfynydd, Penrhyndeudraeth, and over the Snowdon pass, and down at last in the rain to the ancient borough of Caernarvon, and the twenty-acre trial field. It looked an enormous field with its panoply of marquees and tents, parking places, policemen, and notices. Only the *élite* of shepherds and dogs were here to compete, and in fact I

To the Welsh National Trials

had few 'compatriots' from South Wales to keep me company, for the sheeplands of the North naturally supplied the bulk of competitors.

There, however, was David Daniels of Ystradgyn-lais, Breconshire, with Glen and Chip, twice winner of the International Supreme Championship. There was John Evans of Monmouthshire with Nell, Roy and Coon; Tom Cornelius of Ogmore near Bridgend with Craig, Glen and Lad; Gwilym Owen of Brecon with Tot and Nell; Herbert Worthington of Abergavenny with Moss and Floss; and Mervyn Williams of Gladestry with Fan. Arriving with Toss, I completed the hopeful band of South Walians, who together with their few supporters sat on benches boosting their morale with a running crossfire of slanderous insults at each other and each other's dogs. Our nerves were all strung up before the great occasion, and this violent and voluble chaff was the traditional and typical method of relieving the tension as we awaited our turns (though I believe it is less in evidence at English and Scottish competitions).

The comparison between men and dogs stands out in clear contrast at such times. The little Border Collies sit or lie with ears cocked, watching the working of their rivals with a sustained intensity that lasts all day. I have often wondered what goes on inside the chained collie's mind as the sheep move round the course, and his unflinching eyes follow each run from start to finish. Press reporters have fancifully described them as the keenest critics of their rivals' work. My own view is that they are chiefly hypnotised, or something like it, by the movements of the sheep with which their lives and minds are so inextricably bound up.

I had barely half an hour to wait for my turn, and having summed up the course, the behaviour of the sheep, and the difficulties at the end of the deceptive long cross-drive, I took Toss for a little walk. Solitude is good at such times: I would share in the banter of the South Walians afterwards, but for fifteen minutes before my run I wanted to be alone.

Far beyond the field lay the island of Anglesey stretching away to the north, with its happy memories for me of visits in pre-war years, of sketching and story-gathering in the footsteps of George Borrow and Goronwy Owen—Cob Malltraeth, Llanddwyn, and Puffin Island. To the south the mighty ramparts of the Snowdon massif swept upward in grandeur, its sunlit plateaus and shadowy passes bringing also their pleasant memories to fortify me in those fateful minutes before I was called over the loudspeaker by that 'voice of doom'.

The competitor before me, Gwilym Owen, was out on the course and nearing the end of his turn. He had finished penning and was fencing for the final singling thrust to cut out the marked sheep. Was I beginning to lose my nerve? Not on your life. No, I would not admit it to anyone, even to myself, yet my mouth was as dry as chips, and my crook was sticky in my hand. It would have been so easy to nip through the hedge, disappear for half an hour, and return too late to be allowed to run, saving myself the ordeal of having to appear in that great arena; but I looked down into the alert face of little Toss, and his strong brown eyes returned my gaze, radiating confidence, as always when my nerves sagged before a big event.

Suddenly came the burst of applause heralding the end of Gwilym's run. The loudspeaker bawled my name, and the field was mine. Toss looked up at me again, wistful, pensive and very much at the ready. He of course knew well enough what the little walk had meant, the clapping, his name on the loudspeaker. 'What are we waiting for?' he seemed to say.

It was not, however, until Gwilym's sheep had been taken out of sight that I made my appearance, for many a run is spoilt at the start when a young dog is allowed to see the sheep go off back-stage. He will be too interested in their disappearance to locate his distant quarry.

When the field was clear, I strode forward with as bold a show of confidence as I could manage. D. W. Davies of Pontypridd was Course Director and he accompanied me to the starting post, waved his flag for the release of my sheep, then retired. Toss and I were left together, standing in the loneliest place in the world: for the top of Everest must be Piccadilly Circus compared to that spot at the National sheepdog trials with a thousand pairs of eyes at your back, as you wait for the appearance of your sheep with only a little dog, whose brains and training, over the most difficult and subtle animal contest in the world, stand between you and the criticism of the silent audience.

In the stillness of my waiting I faintly heard the word going through the crowd: 'This is the school-master from Cardiff.' Then the five sheep appeared, and were quietly guided into position by the pen men. Toss spotted them and watched intensely, with the motionless gaze of a gargoyle, sitting two yards to my right. The wind of the Irish sea was blowing on his clean white ruff, and the sunlight of Snowdon gleamed on his black coat. The stopwatch clicked and I heard the order: 'Right ho.' I passed it on to the dog, and the static animal was transformed into the character-istic running machine I knew so well. My fifteen minutes were on.

The Cross Drive

He sped away to the right in the usual casting out-run which opened wider and wider, before he closed in for the lift, a little too close behind the sheep for my liking; but they remained calm, and came on steadily between the two poles amidfield with Toss working them. It was perhaps a little jerky, but they moved in a line straight to the spot where I stood; then round the post with Toss on the outside making a splendid turn, before the big test of the drives began.

I tried to cool him down with the aid of the long-practised words; for I could see that he was going to find it hard to restrain his youthful enthusiasm, and to guide the sheep away to pass between the two distant hurdles, the dog *must* walk them calmly. Alas, as I had feared, towards the end of the first drive, his walk gave way to a trot, and this took him *too* close to the sheep, who broke into a run. They veered to the left, and I flanked him to bring them straight again, but a few degrees too far. I flanked him back, he overshot the mark, and before I could get him into position the

sheep were round the hurdles and I had missed. That meant two and a half points down and was enough to put me out of the team, with still a long way to go.

The cross drive followed, probably the most difficult and hazardous item in the whole programme, but also the most thrilling and satisfying thing a trialist can attempt, and, when successfully achieved, the most beautiful spectacle of any trained-animal performance in the world.

After the 'flap' at the end of the first drive, crowd or no crowd, I informed Toss in no uncertain terms exactly what I thought of him. My tone of voice may have sounded murderous enough, but it served its purpose. He took the ninety degree turn and stopped, and the cross drive that followed was a thing of beauty which I shall remember to my dying day. At the right pace, and at the right distance, he took the sheep across the field to pass them between the second pair of hurdles, and then returned them again to where I waited at the edge of the sawdust ring for the next test, the parting or shedding of two sheep from the five.

At this stage you come for the first time face to face with the enemy, for so one comes to regard the five sheep in the shedding. In comparison to your own sheep with their innate good sense and co-operative attitude, the present five are either delinquents or lunatics or both! Normally the shedding-off process is

ιot so very difficult, but in the ring at Caernarvon, as
hose five animals were lined up before me, they
esembled five truculent boys sent in for detention, one
ιr two very anxious to be off, the others submissively
urly.

The plan is to manœuvre them so that a small gap
eparates three from the two to be shed off; the waiting
log is called in swiftly to burst them away like knocked
pples off a spray. We had some difficulty at this stage,
nd for some reason botched it at the first attempt,
arning the loss of a point and a half out of the five;
ιut at the second attempt the shed came off as clean as
whistle.

Then we were off to the pen, which consists of a
ix-foot square enclosure composed of four ordinary
ιurdles, one of which is hinged to form a moving gate
ιith a six-foot length of rope to be held in the hand.

In this pen the sheep must be trapped, and here Toss
ιas few equals. At this stage my five sheep seemed to
ιe in a mood of utter submissiveness, and Toss with
ιis powerful eye had probably almost mesmerised
hem. Under his complete control they walked meekly
ι, and I closed the gate without loss of a point.

One more test remained, to single out the ewe with
he ribbon on its neck. The dog must cut in and force
ιut the one sheep indicated by the crook; then, having
ingled, he must approach resolutely and by the power
ιf his hypnotic glare alone, make the sheep turn round.

(145)   K

The shepherd must on no account help his dog in turning the animal away from its fellows. This is the supreme test of the British Border Collie—no other type of sheepdog can accomplish the task—which entitles it to a special place among dogs and, I would say, above all other animals. There is demonstrated the psychological power of one mind over another! Five points and a twenty-pound prize often hang in the balance at this stage, twenty pounds dangling in the threatening glare of a sheepdog's eye.

Primitive forms of hypnotism are found in cats, weasels, and certain types of snake, but accompanied always by the urge and need to kill; in the Border Collie alone it is found as a harmless manifestation for good, a service to the shepherd, and of economic value to man. Toss, as has been pointed out several times before, had his full share of the strong eye, and by a happy stroke my ewe at Caernarvon was cut out and turned in quick time. The run was over.

The marked sheep stamps defiance on being singled by the dog

To the Welsh National Trials

At a later date my award of points was received from Mr T. H. Halsall, the International Society secretary, and is appended below:

	POINTS	POINTS LOST
Outrun	10	0
Lift	5	$\frac{1}{2}$
Fetch	10	1
Drives	10	4
Shedding	5	$1\frac{1}{2}$
Penning	5	0
Singling	5	0
Style	5	0
Total	55	7

I had lost seven points out of the possible fifty-five, and finished in thirteen minutes. It was not good enough for a place in the National team, but for a two-year-old on his first season I was very well satisfied.

If he lived, Toss would compete at the National for another eight seasons; he was still only a schoolboy and his world was young.

✦✦✦✦✦✦✦✦✦✦✦✦✦✦✦✦✦✦✦✦✦✦✦✦✦✦✦✦✦✦✦✦✦✦✦✦✦✦✦

CHAPTER XV

SEPTEMBER

✦✦✦✦✦✦✦✦✦✦✦✦✦✦✦✦✦✦✦✦✦✦✦✦✦✦✦✦✦✦✦✦✦✦✦✦✦✦✦

The Last Great Test of the Year

THE Christmas term at school was well into its fourth
week, rehearsals for the play had started, the orchestra
was functioning at full blast, and the school societies
were alive once more. Noses were being put to grind-
stones and shoulders to wheels. The University wanted
me to prepare a set of twenty lectures on Natural
History, music was casting its spell upon me once
more, and the world of sheepdogs and trials men had
begun to shrink in importance.

It happened to me each autumn, the transference of
interest from the world of animals to the world of
human beings. The thrills, disappointments, triumphs
and frustrations of the summer season were over, the
wasted sweat, toil and petrol were half forgotten. But
though the trials were over, Toss was still the anchor
by which I was tethered to the game. The season came
to an end, and I was unable to attend the last meetings;
when quite by accident I heard about Llanafan trial in
the remote hill fastnesses of mid-Wales.

I had never been there before, as in previous years my dogs had not been good enough to merit the long trip into the mountains. There was a gruelling test at the end of it, even for the best hill dog; only the finest reached their sheep to gather, and only a small percentage of those returned their charges to the field test at the hurdles. Trialists who had been to Llanafan told grim tales of that fern-clad mountain near the summit of which the sheep were released—and what sheep! The hands of the narrator would rise and fall in anguished frustration at the lack of words with which to describe them.

I gathered that it was the kind of place that respectable trialists only went to once in a lifetime! You were never asked whether you finished the tests or came in the prize list; the only thing which mattered was whether the dog retrieved the sheep. That in itself was sufficient achievement.

Young Toss had already had enough of crowds and car journeys, and this was a trip of nearly a hundred miles from the city to a place where life revolved round the sheep industry. There would be an audience of keener critics than anywhere else, the sheep would be wilder, and the mountain course itself was regarded as the hardest in Wales, the Grand National of the sheepdog world.

Yet somehow the more I thought about it, the more tantalising became the prospect of trying Toss out at

The Last Great Test of the Year

Llanafan. There would be no more competitions until the following summer, so the die was cast. I decided to go.

★

It was a hazy morning of light mist and heavy dew, and as I drove northward there was a look of smug satisfaction from my back-seat passenger. Here was yet another trip, one more thrill, one more gasp of the breath of life, one more glorious day away from our respective kennels. The sun came out, and the clouds with their shadows raced by across the dying grass of the Beacons.

Beyond Brecon town I turned for Pont faen and the home of Gwilym Owen, master of Rhiw Goch, Llan-fihangel-nant-Brân, to give it its full and glorious title. Gwilym was a successful trialist and a noted breeder and show-winner of Radnor sheep; I was anxious to see the rams of his breed.

He was expecting me, and after lunch we climbed into his Landrover, where Toss shared the back with his two beautiful bitches, Nell and Tot.

By narrow country lanes, winding and twisting, rising and falling, we came at last to the edge of the lonely Eppynt mountains. My friend was anxious to show me some rams which belonged to his uncle, Rees Lewis, whose farmstead nestled in one of the countless valleys leading out of Eppynt. We arrived there, and Lewis took us to a tiny field where the seven grey-faced patriarchs of his flock were enclosed until the mating season (which comes late in the mountains).

We caught and handled all seven. They were not the pampered animals you often see at ram sales, fattened on clover, oats and cake, brushed, trimmed and washed before they appeared in the selling ring. Here instead was the real thing, with no pretensions at being something else: a group of hill rams straight off the fern, hard and splendid in their natural setting.

One of them particularly had caught my eye from the beginning: a hornless two-year-old, short in the leg and neck, a neat head, a tight coat of wool and a firm body. He would be ideal for fat lambs on the gentler hills of my South Glamorgan district. It was some while before Lewis divulged the price of this ram, and he and his nephew continued thereafter to exchange good-natured banter about the merits and demerits of their respective stock; so I meanwhile had plenty of time to think over my prospective purchase. At last I decided that the price was right, whereupon I clinched the deal, and arrangements were made for the ram's dispatch southwards.

With the ending of the trials season, and the buying of a new ram, the shepherd's year both ends and starts again: the alpha and omega of the hill harvest. With the selling of the last of the lamb crop come the nuptials for the next year's crop—the autumn mating period for the ewes, with this grey-faced Radnor to sire my flock. A five-months pregnancy would lead to the birth of lambs to coincide with the stirring of young grass. (Baby lambs must have such grass, which also helps lactation in the ewes.) Then, in the winds of March and showers of April, little grey-faced lambs would meet on their ancient prancing grounds above the Nofydd Valley, and frisk about while their short lives lasted.

The afternoon was far advanced as we took our leave, and turned on to the moorland road. On all sides the rolling hills, covered with half-dead fern and heather, rose and fell away towards the far horizons, and the air was good to breathe. We talked still about only one subject, we one-track-mindsters, and that was the trial season ending that day, and the successes and failures of our rivals.

We passed the ancient ruined hostelry, Drover's Arms, standing like an oasis half-way across that lonely place—the old grey sentinel recalling the past, when long lines of cattle droves passed on their way to the industrial south.

After some miles of the fresh and tranquil uplands, we overtook a big grey shooting brake. 'I'll bet that's Tom Cornelius,' said Gwilym. He was quite right, the well-known Bridgend trialist was also bound for Llanafan; but with only one of his dogs in the back instead of the usual four—here was a mystery which puzzled us. Soon, however, we passed his young son,

Colin, with two dogs on the leash, and the mystery was over. They had obviously been exercising the dogs on the moorland road.

Before dropping down to the valley of the Irfon and the world of fields and men once more, we paused at the head of the valley to admire the view. Then Tom overtook us and stopped. 'I've lost Lad,' he said, and told us how he had stopped to release the dogs, and one of them had suddenly and unaccountably slipped away.

What could have prompted him to turn a deaf ear to his master's whistles, to take off into the moors and disappear? This was no instance of stupidity, Cornelius's Lad was one of the best dogs in the game. Nor (as some might guess if they did not know the man) had he been given a thrashing; for Tom would no more have struck that dog than I would have beaten Toss. It seemed more probable that the sudden revelation of the mountain spaces after the closed car had awoken in Lad an irresistible and age-old urge to find his freedom. We could only guess at an answer, but the plain fact was that the moors had claimed Tom's finest winning dog, and nothing could be done about it: some power far stronger than his beloved master's whistles must have drawn him away.

Poor bereft Tom, now tired of his hopeless search, went on towards the trials, while we drove back some way and stopped at the highest point to scan the sur-

rounding hills for a glimpse of the dog. Suddenly
Gwilym's practised eye picked out a faint white blur a
mile away, where a group of sheep were bunched together. Instantly we knew that a dog would be there
holding them. When we reached the place, he stood
up and eyed us critically, but however carefully we
tried to coax him, there was nothing doing: he shyly
turned away and disappeared over the rising ground,
and we continued once more towards Llanafan. That
evening, however, Tom Cornelius, returning home,
found his dog waiting on the road near the place where
he had been released many hours before.

At last we reached the trial ground, where, in a little
field at the foot of Bwlch Ciliau mountain, a miniature
agricultural show was being held. Rows of gigantic
swedes and mangolds shone in the fading autumn sunshine, and 'dolled-up' mountain rams and lambs stood
reluctant and silent in their hurdle pens. Gay little
mountain ponies were showing off their paces before
an admiring crowd.

How people could attach importance to such things
when they could see a sheepdog working on the side
of the mountain, was beyond me. Here was being
enacted one of the world's great tests of animal behaviour. This was no ordinary field trial, where the
dogs merely simulate the gathering off the hill for the
convenience of spectators. This was the real thing, and
I saw that my friends had not exaggerated.

Sheepdog Glory

As each dog left the field, a buttress of the hill concealed the sheep from its sight. The shepherd could sometimes help his dog to find by guiding him on with whistled orders. This was only possible with experienced hill dogs accustomed to going up mountain sides 'blind' and running to orders. The regular trials men, who trained their dogs for competitions only, fell by the wayside. As each of their dogs ran out and the distance increased, misunderstandings became obvious. One after another, the dogs failed to make the distance, and had to be called in.

At last my turn came, the last run of the year, and I was confident that Toss would reach the mountain top. I walked to the starting point as the course director waved his flag—in signal to the poor wretches at the summit to release the sheep. Three white dots appeared against the autumn sky, and Toss paused in his walk beside me to the starting post. I was happy then in the knowledge that he would 'find' in the minimum of time and without assistance from me.

I had always considered it to be a good policy in training to give a priming order to my dogs, to help them to sight their sheep and anticipate the eagerly awaited command to go. If human athletes on the mark before a race need this priming order to 'get ready', 'get set', how much more necessary is this in the case of an animal!

'Can you see them, Toss?' I whispered, realising

(156)

subconsciously the twofold absurdity of the question, since I knew he had seen them, and in any case he could not answer me! Then followed the whistle which released the tension in his frame and gave him the glorious freedom to obey his long-suppressed instincts. Now he was at last allowed to run over the field and up the mountain side, with that single-minded purposefulness for which he was already becoming famous among my rivals. Toss was away on his last trial run of the year—and what a run it was!

It was long odds on any dog being able to find his sheep without directions from the shepherd. For the lowland one-field trials, we had never had occasion to learn this long-range language of the hills. To succeed at Llanafan, man and dog would have to be 'bilingual' with one set of orders for close-range work, and a considerably magnified set of whistled commands audible and workable at a mile away.

Toss left the field and took to the hill as a falcon takes to the sky, and the tiny black speck of him grew smaller and smaller as he curved steadily on the lower side of the hill. For upwards of three-quarters of a mile he ran, as if nursing a clear mental image of the point he was making for, and my heart went with him in his final trials flight towards his goal at the summit.

The mountain received his tiny running form, the steep rough grass and fern and rock seemed only to increase the violence of his urge to reach the distant spot where the sheep were standing. To him the stones and heather were as branches to a squirrel, or as breakers to a seal. On and up he sped, for the elemental impulse to run and gather for his master had taken possession of him wholly.

Behind me, in their leggings, mackintoshes and bowler hats, the crowd stood silent. This was no audience of spell-bound townsfolk, wondering at the trial dog's skill. They were all hill farmers, tough life-long critics of the working of sheepdogs. They watched in silence as the schoolmaster's dog from the city soared into his natural element, the birthright of his ancient breed and calling. Being shepherds, whose daily task involved the long drag for the half-wild sheep of mid-Wales, they knew and felt, with the instinctive knowledge of such men, that here was a dog with all the gifts of vision and determination for these exacting conditions.

A hundred yards from the summit the moving spot veered slightly into the familiar cast. Toss had sighted his sheep again, and had swung behind them and stopped before my long four-finger whistle reached him. Lungs and voice were of no avail at that great distance; he was on his own up there, beyond the reach of our 'monoglot' one-field conversation. It was a far cry from that memorable day at Harold Hawken's place when the mind of the frail and sickly pup had overcome his physical weakness to give me a glimpse of the great style and beauty which might be in him.

From his commanding position behind his sheep, he started the 'lift', and the downward cavalcade began. Steadily at first, but for some reason the ewes took fright, and the rot set in. Too fast, too fast! A long blast checked his urgent follow, but the sheep came on. It was no good leaving him up there, and trying to stop the wild sheep by myself. Toss was now within shouting range, so I called him on. He took the command eagerly, probably well aware that his poor benighted boss, with all the human aid on Llanafan show field, would never stop his quarry from gaining their liberty. The most dreaded commandment in the Border Collie's calendar might have come to his mind: 'Thou shalt not lose thy master's sheep.'

They entered the field at a gallop, led by a big horned wether ram with head held high. All up now, I thought, but even as they careered past me, they were passed and hooked by the little collie, cornered again and stopped at every turn, till they eventually steadied down. The two ewes were at last persuaded to pass between the parallel hurdles, but the wily ram kept outside until the third attempt, when all three went meekly through and on into the little pen—as the time-keeper stopped his watch and my trials season came to an end.

Toss was the third dog to pen his sheep that day,

but we could not wait for the verdict. The long road through the mountain darkness claimed us, and towards the end Toss lay on the seat beside me with his head and paw across my thigh, fast asleep. Occasionally my left hand would slip from the steering wheel to fondle a limp and silky ear: what after all did the prize money mean to either of us! And long after midnight, when I put him in his bed of straw, he looked into the beam of my torch, his brown eyes steady as a lioness, and he seemed to be saying: 'There will be more triumphs some day.'

But whatever the future holds for him, the image of that final run of the year, and how small the mountain was made to look by Toss's tiny racing figure, will remain with me, unforgettably, for life.

Lightning Source UK Ltd.
Milton Keynes UK
UKOW03f2054131014

240059UK00001B/27/P